Contents

A STRAIGHTFORWARD GUIDE

TO

UNDERSTANDING AND CONTROLLING

INHERITANCE TAX

David Marsh

Editor: Roger Sproston

Straightf

www.straig

Straightforward Guides

ISBN
978-1-80236-228-2

Printed by 4Edge Ltd www.4Edge.co.uk

Cover design by BW- studio Derby

Whilst every effort has been made to ensure that the information contained within this book is correct at the time of going to press, the author and publisher can take no responsibility for any errors and omissions contained within.

Introduction

This book has been updated to 2023. However, as a cautionary note, given the changing nature of rules and regulations and also budgets, it is always best to double check figures relating to inheritance tax and taxation rates generally by using the government and HMRC websites.

The subject of inheritance tax is an emotive one, in that most people choose not to think about it and elect to get on with their lives instead. However, particularly as we get older, it is never quite that simple and a degree of forward planning is necessary if one is to avoid relatives and loved ones paying high levels of inheritance tax after death.

The Office of Tax Simplification

In 2018 the Office of Tax Simplification carried out a survey, taking on board comments by 3500 members of the public. Among the conclusions were that 'inheritance tax seems to be the most uniquely unpopular tax'. People responses included "this tax is unforgiving when you are at your lowest and most vulnerable". "I still have nightmares about it" and "the Burden of form-filling is a tax in itself".

The first part of the report was published in November 2018, and the second part in 2019, The first part looks at the administration of the tax and the second part looks at how it is structured and who pays what. The first report suggests that inheritance tax greatly adds to the burden on people who are trying to sort out matters following a death. The key recommendation here is that the government introduces a simple, streamlined, digital system for inheritance tax and probate. This would cut down the information required from the 95% of estates not liable for inheritance tax. Currently, there are about 20 different forms used in the process. It also suggests introducing automatic receipts for forms and money sent to the tax office. Others complain that the tax-free allowance on gifts has not kept pace with inflation, that people without spouses and children have fewer reliefs, particularly on property and that the wealthy don't pay their fair share of the tax. For a fuller overview of the report go to: www.gov.uk/government/publications/office-of-tax-simplification-inheritance-tax-review

One area that has been affected, which will be outlined in chapter eight, is the way inheritance tax has been affected by the pension reforms of 2015. Basically, this allows people who die before the age of 75 to pass on pension pots to beneficiary's tax free and subsequent draw downs will also be tax free. Where someone dies after age 75, tax due on the pension fund will be determined by the income tax position of the person inheriting the pension. This could be 0, 20, 40 or 45 per cent, depending on their tax band.

How to protect your loved ones from inheritance tax

All of what is described below will be covered in more detail throughout the book. A summary of the main points is presented here:

- Use your main IHT exemption. The first £325,000 of your estate-the nil-rate band is exempt from inheritance tax Above that your estate is taxed at a flat 40%. married couples and those in civil partnerships can pass everything on to each other without tax, including the allowance. It was announced in the Finance Bill 2021 that Inheritance Tax nil rate bands will remain at existing levels until April 2026.

- Use the residence nil-rate band (RNRB) which allows you to hand an additional £175,000 slice of the family home to direct descendant's tax free which, when added to the £325,000 nil-rate band, means that £500,000 of your estate could escape IHT. The RNRB is transferable between spouses and civil partners so a couple can shelter up to £1,000,000 of their estate if leaving to direct dependants.

- Write life insurance policies in trust. Transferring a policy to the care of a second party (a trustee) for the benefit of a third party (a beneficiary) will put it outside your estate and not liable for tax. Your insurer will be able to provide you with a form.

- Make use of annual allowances. You can give away £3,000 a year without it becoming liable for IHT later on. This £3,000 can be divided between as many people as you like. On top of this you can give small gifts of up to £250 to as many people as you wish. You can also give £1,000 per person as a wedding gift, £5,000 to a child and £2,500 to a grandchild. Larger gifts of unlimited amounts can be tax-free as long as you live for seven years after making them. You can also make regular gifts from income, not capital, as long as they do not affect your standard of living. It is important to keep records of income, expenditure and gifts so that your family can claim exemption after death.

- Money left in a pension is normally IHT free. It can make sense to spend other savings and investments before taking money from your pension. The pension IHT rules mean that you can build up £1,073.100 which can be passed on tax free. As stated above, if the person passing on the pension pot dies before the age of 75 there will be no tax to pay when the recipient starts drawing money from the pot. If a person dies after 75 there will be a recipient tax at their highest marginal rate.

Inheritance tax is a technical and complex area or can be. Most people have a very basic understanding of the main facts, such as the inheritance tax level and so on. The purpose of this book is to enable the reader to understand the complexities and to make informed decisions about their assets and the best way to organise these assets to avoid paying exorbitant levels of tax.

The subject of inheritance tax is approached logically. Firstly, the nature of inheritance tax is outlined and also how we work out inheritance tax. Assets are then explored and placed in the context of working out inheritance tax liabilities. The practice of reserving gifts is explored and we also look at the various inheritance tax reliefs available.

We look at responsibility for inheritance tax and the ways in which we can further reduce the tax burden. Finally, we look at the process of probate and the importance of making a will. Overall, the reader will gain an invaluable insight into inheritance tax and how to plan so that excessive tax is avoided.

This book deals with the law as it affects the United Kingdom, as laws affecting the Channel Islands and the Isle of Man are different.

In addition, for further information concerning Scotland and Northern Ireland go to:
https://www.mygov.scot/inheritance-tax-support and:
https://northern-ireland.directwillstrusts.co.uk/inheritance-tax

****

Chapter 1

Explaining Inheritance Tax-General Principles

In this chapter we will be looking at the following areas:

- Definition of inheritance tax (IHT)
- The law underpinning IHT
- The concept of domicile and IHT
- The making of gifts and transfers of value
- Items excluded from IHT
- Items that attract IHT
- Exempt gifts

A definition of inheritance tax

Inheritance tax is, basically, a tax on giving before death in the form of gifts or after death through a will or through the administration of a person's affairs if a will is not left. For general purposes, anything over £325,000 (2023-2024) is payable at 40% or 36% if the estate qualifies for a reduced rate as a result of a charitable donation. There are a number of ways to minimise inheritance tax liability as we will see.

Increased threshold for married couples and civil partners

Married couples and registered civil partners can effectively increase the threshold on their estate when the second partner dies. (£650,000 2023/24) (or £1m if the estate includes a home). Their executors or personal representatives must transfer the first spouse or civil partner's unused Inheritance Tax threshold or 'nil rate band' to the second spouse or civil partner when they die.

The Legislation covering inheritance tax

The law governing inheritance tax is based on the Inheritance Tax Act 1984 as amended. Fundamentally, inheritance tax becomes payable after death or when there is what is known as a *transfer of value* as the result of a transfer of property (such as the making of a gift or gifts) or a failure to act, unless the transfer or failure is within one of the exemptions allowed for, which will be outlined later. In this case it is known as an exempt disposition.

A transfer is also exempt if the property in respect of which the transfer takes place is an *excluded property* or excluded gift.

The tax payable is less if the inheritance reliefs specified in the Act notionally reduce either the value of the property or the tax itself.

The Concept of Domicile

Although there are other taxes, none of these are affected by domicile as is IHT (domicile or tax residence arises if the taxpayer has his or her residence in the state where he or she spends most of their time). If a taxpayer has his or her residence in the United Kingdom, or is deemed to have it there, inheritance tax is charged whenever there is a gratuitous transfer of value (other than exemptions) in respect of assets in whatever country they may be.

If the taxpayer's domicile is outside the UK, the tax only applies to those assets that are situated in the UK. A person will have his or her domicile in the state which he considers to be his permanent home, even though he might not have the right of residence there.

For inheritance tax purposes it is important to understand the nature of domicile. At birth, a person will have the domicile of his mother if he is illegitimate or his father is dead, other wise he will have the domicile of his father. A person can exchange the domicile of origin (or birth) for one of choice once over the age of 16 and mentally capable. If there is an intention to live there indefinitely, whether legally or not, then this will be deemed to be the domicile of choice. If a person is dependent on another, whether mentally incapable or under 16, this will be known as a domicile of dependency.

Deemed domicile

Another important concept is one of deemed domicile. Even if you are not domiciled in the UK under general law, the Revenue will treat you as domiciled in the UK for inheritance tax ("IHT") if at the date of your death:

- You were domiciled in the UK within the three years immediately before death, or
- You were resident in the UK for income tax purposes for at least 15 out of the last 20 years ending with the year in which you died.
- If you were born in the UK with a domicile of origin but acquire a domicile of choice elsewhere, you will be deemed domiciled in the UK for all tax purposes once you have been a UK resident for at least one of the last two years.
- If you are domiciled or deemed domiciled in the UK, then IHT applies to your worldwide assets.
- If you are not domiciled or deemed domiciled in the UK, then IHT applies only to your UK assets.

Where assets pass from a UK domiciled spouse/civil partner to a non-UK domiciled spouse/civil partner, the spouse exemption is limited to Nil Rate Band, £325,000 (2023/2024) (in addition to any available nil rate band).

Inheritance tax and transfers of value

The Inheritance Tax Act 1984 defines transfer of value as 'a disposition by a person...as a result of which the value of his estate immediately after the disposition is less than it would be but for the disposition; and the amount by which it is less is the 'value transferred' by the transfer'.

Deciphering this, calculation of inheritance tax is based upon the reduction the transaction causes to the wealth of the giver and not the increase in the recipient's wealth.

Taxable and non-taxable giving

Some transactions which cause a reduction in the taxpayer's wealth are declared by the Act as not to be transfers of value and therefore are exempt. Section 10 of the Inheritance Tax Act 1984 states 'A disposition which is not intended...to confer any gratuitous benefit and which is either entered into at arms length between 'persons not connected with each other' or which is 'such as might be expected to be' entered into at 'arms length between persons not connected with each other' is not taxable.

Persons connected with each other for this purpose are the taxpayer's family including spouse or civil partner, ancestors, lineal descendants, brothers and sisters, uncles and aunts, nephews and nieces, the spouse or the civil partner of the above family members and the relatives in the same categories of the taxpayer's spouse or civil partner.

Except in respect of commercial transactions relating to partnership assets, the taxpayer's business partner and the partners spouse or registered civil partner are also considered to be connected to him.

In addition, transfers made during the taxpayer's lifetime in favour of a spouse, registered civil partner or a child of the taxpayer or child of his spouse or registered civil partner, for the purpose of family maintenance are exempt.

This exemption applies not only during the subsistence of the relationship but also in respect of arrangements made on the annulment or dissolution of the relationship. It also provides for transfers for the reasonable maintenance of a dependant relative. In the case of a child, it only applies to transfers of value for the maintenance, education or training of the child until he attains 18 years of age or until he ceases full time education if later.

One other exemption is the grant of an agricultural tenancy for full consideration, payable in money or moneys worth.

Property excluded from inheritance tax

Certain property (property is not limited to bricks and mortar) is not liable to incur inheritance tax as below:

- Savings Certificates and Premium bonds owned by people who are domiciled in the Channel Islands or the Isle of Man.
- Certain British Government stock owned by those living abroad.
- Certain overseas pensions and lump sums payable on death.
- Emoluments and tangible movable property which is owned by visiting armed forces.
- Property of service people who die as a result of active military service.
- By concession, decorations awarded for valour or gallantry which have never been transferred in return for money or moneys worth. The decoration need not have been solely a medal or remain in the same family.
- Property situated outside the United Kingdom which belongs to a person who is domiciled outside of the United Kingdom.
- Foreign currency bank accounts with most banks in the UK that are held by people who are of foreign domicile and who are not resident or ordinarily resident in the UK.
- Most reversionary interests, i.e. most presently owned rights to property upon the death of someone who is currently entitled to their property during their lifetime under a trust.

Assets that incur inheritance tax liability

The assets that attract inheritance tax liability (unless excluded) are as follows:

- Everything that the taxpayer owns (including shares of property co-owned with someone else.
- Everything that he has given away in the last seven years of his life unless they are exempted gifts.
- Every non-exempt gift he has made from which he has reserved a right to benefit in the last seven years.
- Everything owned by someone else from which the taxpayer is entitled to benefit for the remainder of the taxpayer's life or for any other limited period (known as a life tenancy) or the assets of any trust fund of which the taxpayer has a right to the income for the rest of his life, if-
- the life tenant was entitled as a disabled person under a trust for the disabled (see chapter on trusts)
- the life tenancy was created by a will or intestacy and began immediately upon the death, or-
- the life tenancy was created by an arrangement or trust created before 22 March 2006, or
- the life tenancy follows immediately upon a life tenancy in existence on April 6th, 2006, that ended before April 6th 2008, or

- the life tenant was the spouse or the civil partner of a person who was a life tenant under a pre-April 2006 trust at that date who died on or after 6th April 2008 and the life tenant's entitlement immediately followed on that of his spouse or civil partner, or
- the life tenancy is the first or a subsequent life tenancy in a trust created before 22nd March 2006 which is a trust of a life policy or life policies, provided that there has been no break in the sequence of life tenancies.

1, 2 and 3 above are known as the taxpayer's free estate and 4 as the settled estate. From the total of these assets, it is permissible to deduct the debts and financial liabilities transferred with the assets to which they relate and if the transfer of value takes place as a result of the taxpayer's death, the amount of the taxpayer's debts and reasonable funeral expenses. However, if the taxpayer is insolvent, it is not allowed to deduct any deficiency in the free estate from the settled estate.

Gifts that are exempt

Gifts that are exempt from inheritance tax are the following:

- Gifts made by the taxpayer more than seven years prior to his death without retaining any benefit from the gift unless the gift is made to a company or a trust (other than a trust for the disabled). These gifts are known as immediately chargeable gifts. With the exception of immediately chargeable gifts, gifts only remain potentially liable to inheritance tax for the seven years after they have been made and are known as PET's (Potentially exempt transfers). If the donor survives the making of a PET by seven years the PET is exempt from IT. Gifts that count as a PET are gifts that you, as an individual, make to another individual, a trust for someone who is disabled or a bereaved minor's trust. This is where, as the beneficiary of an Interest in possession Trust you decide to give up the right to receive anything from that trust or that right comes to an end for any other reason during your lifetime. See chapter on trusts.

- Gifts of any amount to a spouse or civil partner, unless the taxpayer is domiciled in the UK, but the spouse or civil partner is not, in which case the exemption is limited to £55,000.

- Gifts of not more than £3000 in total made in any tax year during the lifetime of the taxpayer. Any unused benefit from this exemption can be carried forward for one tax year and the annual exemption for any current tax year is used up before the unused balance of the annual exemption from any previous tax year.

- Gifts made during the taxpayer's lifetime which are made as part of the normal expenditure of the taxpayer out of his income and not from capital and which do not reduce his standard of living. Normal expenditure is expenditure which is in accordance with a settled pattern of the donor's expenditure.

- Wedding gifts made before the ceremony during the taxpayer's lifetime, up to £5,000 to his child, up to £2,500 to his grandchild and up to £1000 in the case of anyone else.

- Gifts made in the taxpayer's lifetime for the maintenance of a spouse, ex spouse, civil partner, ex civil partner, dependant relatives and dependant children who are under the age of 18 or are in full time education.

- Gifts to registered charities for charitable purposes.

- Gifts for certain national purposes including gifts to most museums and art galleries and to political parties which have at least two sitting members of the House of Commons or which have one sitting member and whose candidate polled 150,000 votes at the next general election.

- Gifts of land to registered housing associations.

- Gifts in any number of the above classes can be made to the same person without losing the benefit of the exemption and under the small gift's exemption any number of gifts up to £250 can be made in a tax year provided that no other gift has been made to the same person in the same tax year. If the sum given under the small gift's exemption exceeds £250 the benefit of the exemption is lost and the entire amount is taxable.

Married people and those with registered civil partners should remember that each spouse and civil partner has a separate set of gift exemptions. The percentage of the value of any gift which is not an exempt disposition or gift of excluded property that is extracted as tax, i.e., the rate of tax charged, is dependent upon whether the gift is deemed to have been made at the time of the taxpayers death or whether it was made during his life and if so how long he survived the making of the gift. It also depends on who or what organisation was the recipient of the gift and the type of property given. It is therefore essential to ensure that full documentary evidence which shows dates and value of all gifts is kept, plus when they were made.

****

Chapter 2

Inheritance Tax Calculations

In this chapter we look at the following:

- The IHT tax threshold
- Calculation of IHT payable on gifts in life
- Calculation of IHT on gifts in death
- Immediately chargeable lifetime gifts

As mentioned, each year the government creates a tax threshold, which is a sum below which no inheritance tax is payable. Currently in 2023/2024 this is £325,000. It has been at this level since 2011 and will remain so until 2026 when it is further reviewed. Therefore, if your estate is less than this amount no tax will be payable. The band below £325,000 is known as the nil-rate band. The rate applicable to lifetime chargeable lifetime gifts in excess of the nil-rate band is 20% and the rate applicable to chargeable transfers on death above the nil-rate band is 40%.

Note that current rules also mean that the survivor of a marriage or a civil partnership can benefit from up to double the inheritance tax allowance-£650,000 (2023/24). You can only transfer threshold if:

- the couple were married or in a civil partnership when the first death occurred.
- you send the request to HMRC within 2 years of the death of the surviving spouse or civil partner.

Where one party to a marriage or civil partnership dies and does not use their nil-rate band to make tax free bequests to other members of the family, the unused amount can be transferred and used by the survivor's estate on their death.

As we have mentioned, gifts and transfers of value are valued for inheritance tax purposes at the amount by which the estate of the person making the transfer is diminished as a result of the transfer and not by the amount by which the recipient or any other person benefits from the transfer.

Inheritance tax on gifts in life

To calculate the amount of inheritance tax payable on a gift made during life you should:

1. total all the chargeable transfers of value made by the giver within the previous seven tax years excluding any exempt gifts and excluded property.

2. deduct any debts and financial liabilities which are transferred with the asset to which the debt or financial liability relates.
3. deduct the balance of the tax threshold which remains unused by previous non-exempt gifts made in the previous seven years.
4. apply the full lifetime rate of tax to the resultant figure.
5. if the transfer was made more than three years before death, apply taper relief to the amount of tax (see further on in the book)

Inheritance tax payable on death

To calculate IT payable on the estate following death, add the total of the net death estate to the total of the chargeable lifetime gifts made in the previous seven years and deduct any balance of the tax threshold which has not been used in respect of lifetime gifts. Apply the full death tax rate to this figure and then deduct the full tax payable on the lifetime gifts. There are permissible deductions when calculating the net estate on death:

- any legacies which are exempt gifts, e.g., legacies to a spouse or to a registered charity for its charitable purposes.
- reasonable funeral and mourning expenses including the cost of a memorial.

- any debts and liabilities existing at the date of death for which the taxpayer had received value or that were imposed by law, e.g., outstanding income tax.
- the cost of realising or administering any property which is situated outside the United Kingdom up to 50% of its value.
- excluded property.

Calculating the nil-rate band which remains available on death

Any non-exempt gift (other than excluded property) made in the seven years before a death is deducted from the tax exemption threshold available to be set against the net estate at death by the value transferred by the gift.

Calculating the nil-rate band when making an immediately chargeable lifetime gift.

When dealing with immediately chargeable lifetime gifts (gifts made during life to trusts, other than trusts for the benefit of disabled beneficiaries or to companies), to calculate the value of the inheritance tax exemption threshold which can be set against the gift, it is necessary to deduct from the then current IT threshold figure the total value of all immediately chargeable gifts made by the giver in the last seven years. If the total value of the immediately chargeable gifts made in the previous seven years and the current gift exceeds the current tax threshold, tax is payable on the excess. Gifts other than immediately chargeable gifts are ignored and are not deducted from the threshold figure when calculating how much of the nil-rate band remains and is available to set off against an immediately chargeable gift, because being PET's, they are still potentially exempt and not chargeable.

Gifts are treated as being deducted in chronological order in which they are made. For example, if a gift of £200,000 is made two years before death to A and one year later £200,000 is gifted to B the gift to A will be exempt from tax but B may well be charged tax, depending on the amount of threshold at the date of death.

If the total value of immediately chargeable non-exempt gifts made in the previous seven years and the value of the immediately chargeable gift currently being made exceeds the then tax threshold, inheritance tax (at one half the rate in respect of gifts made on death) is immediately payable on the excess. Credit is given on death for tax that has been paid on immediately chargeable gifts made in the previous seven years, but if the tax paid exceeds the tax payable on them at death the excess is not repayable.

Has as been previously outlined, transfers made more than seven years before death are exempt transfers. Transfers made in the seven years immediately preceding death are potentially exempt until death occurs unless they are immediately chargeable gifts. Transfers other than immediately chargeable transfers are not taken into account when calculating the tax payable on immediately chargeable transfers until death occurs when a revision of the tax might or might not become necessary, depending how long has elapsed between the transfer and death.

****

Chapter 3

Valuing Assets

In this chapter we cover the following:

- The calculation of asset value
- Grossing up profits

Calculating assets

We will also cover this area in the final chapters of the book when dealing with probate.

Assets are valued for the purposes of IHT at their open market value. Rules exist to assist HMRC in valuing assets.

Valuation of unit trusts, corporate bonds and other stock

As is well known, unit trusts have two values, one at which managers are willing to sell units and the lower price at which managers are willing to buy them back. For IT purposes, unit trusts are valued at the lower of the prices. Corporate bonds and other stock also have a buying price and a lower selling price The taxpayer can choose which of these two figures he will use, as opposed to HMRC.

Valuations of stocks and shares for IT purposes can be obtained from most banks and stockbrokers or from www.sharedata.co.uk and there is a charge for this information.

If a share has been quoted 'ex-dividend' the dividend which has been declared must be included in the valuation for inheritance tax purposes: if debenture or loan stock is quoted ex-interest, the interest (less tax at the appropriate rate) must be included.

Stocks and shares that are not quoted

The basis upon which stocks and shares that are not quoted on a recognised stock exchange are valued will depend on the percentage of the company's share capital held by the taxpayer. A Shareholding of 50% or less is valued according to the dividend yield. A holding of between 50% and 90% on an earnings yield and a holding of 90% or over on an asset basis.

Life policies

If the life policy is valued at the time of death the value is the sum paid out by the assurance company. If the transfer occurs on any other occasion the value is the open market value at which the policy could be sold (not the surrender value).

Property that is related

Related property is property which would have an increased value if owned with other property that is:

- owned by the taxpayer's spouse or civil partner, or
- was owned within the last five years by a charity, housing authority, political party which qualifies for exempt transfers or an institution in the amended schedule 3 of the Inheritance Tax Act 1986, to which it was transferred by the taxpayer or his spouse or civil partner after April 15th, 1976.

There are two methods of valuing related property-the general method and the special rule method. The general rule method is used when items of related property have different attributes. The special method is used when property has identical attributes.

Land, shares, and other sold within a short time of death

If the value of shares (other than those quoted on the Alternative Investment market AIM), unit trusts, common investment funds and land or buildings fall during the period of administration of an estate, and in the course of the administration they are sold to a beneficiary at a loss, compared to their value at the date of death, then it is perfectly reasonable to have the value revised to reflect the fall. This reduced value will also become the base cost for capital gains purposes.

To obtain an agreement by HMRC to a revaluation in the case of stock exchange securities and unit trusts, the personal representatives must have sold them within 12 months of the date of death. If the personal representatives reinvest the proceeds of sale by buying further unit trusts or quoted investments within two months of the last sale during the 12-month period, the amount of repayable tax will be restricted.

Similar principles apply in the case of land or buildings, the main difference being that the period of sale is four years instead of 12 months.

The period for reinvestment is four months after the last qualifying sale in the period of four years from death instead of two months during the period of 12 months from death and sales at a profit in the fourth year after death or which result in a profit or loss of less than 5% or £1,000 whichever is the lower, are ignored.

Grossing up gifts

Inheritance tax payable on immediately chargeable lifetime gifts is payable by the donor unless agreed otherwise. If the tax is paid by the donor the gift must be 'grossed up' for the purpose of calculating inheritance tax. This means that the gift is considered to be the amount of the gift and the tax because that is the amount by which the donor's wealth has diminished. If additional tax is paid because the donor dies within seven years of making the gift, it is always paid by the donee.

Rates of inheritance tax and any allowances and exemptions can be found on HMRC website www. hmrc.gov.uk.

****

Chapter 4

The Pre-owned Assets Tax Charge

In this chapter will look at:

- The reservation of benefits
- The pre-owned assets income tax charge
- Calculation of the charge
- Exceptions to the charge

Reserving benefits

If a gift is made but a benefit is reserved by the giver, for example the continued use of a house or other property, the asset is still deemed to be part of the taxpayer's estate as long as he derives benefit from it or is entitled to benefit from it without making any payment for the use or benefit at a full commercial rate. The gift is not deemed to have been fully made until the donee takes full possession of it.

Not surprisingly, HMRC takes a strict view of what exactly constitutes reservation of benefit and considers there is a reservation of benefit in any case where the benefit is significant in relation to the property given.

An example might be the use of a house that has been gifted. Once the house is gifted, HMRC would see very occasional use by the donor as not constituting a reservation but frequent use would. It is wise, in the long run, to avoid making or creating any form of reservation once property of any description is gifted.

Pre-owned assets tax charge

As might be imagined, people come up with various diverse and complicated schemes to avoid inheritance tax liability resulting from gifts with reservation. However, HMRC, as usual, is on the case. In the budget of March 2004, the then Chancellor Gordon Brown outlined proposals for what is known as the 'free standing income tax charge' based on pre-owned assets to counteract these schemes and 'the benefit that people get from having free or low-cost enjoyment of assets they formerly owned or provided funds to purchase'. Basically, if a scheme succeeds in the avoidance of inheritance tax liability that results from the reservation of benefit rules, then liability for income tax is likely to be incurred under the pre-owned assets charge.

The pre-owned assets charge is similar in nature to tax paid by employees for benefits in kind supplied by their employees. A financial sum is attributed to the benefit and tax is paid accordingly. Cash value benefits under £5,000 are disregarded. This law came into being from 6th April 2005 and applies to all gifts made after 17th March 1986.

The charge applies to both tangible and intangible assets. It also applies to any funds or contributions to funds used to acquire the assets from which the donor benefits and whether the funds or contributions are directly or indirectly provided.

In the case of those who are deemed to domiciled in the United Kingdom, the charge applies to assets held anywhere in the world and in the case of anyone else only to their assets in the UK.

Calculating the tax charge

The amount of tax payable is a sum equivalent to the annual rental value of the asset in the case of land or buildings and in the case of other assets to a rate of interest on a notional loan of a sum equal to the market value of the asset, and in each case less any payment made under a legally binding agreement for the use of the asset.

After the deduction of the amount paid for the benefit, the sum so ascertained is added to the taxpayer's taxable income and taxed at his top rate of tax. The first £5,000 per annum is ignored but once the £5,000 is exceeded the exemption is totally lost.

*

The current charges are set out in:
www.gov.uk/hmrc-internal-manuals/inheritance-tax-manual/ihtm44026

Exceptions

As usual there are exceptions to the above charge as follows:

- the asset ceased to be owned before March 18th, 1986.
- the formerly owned asset is currently owned by the taxpayer's civil partner or spouse.
- the asset was transferred to a spouse, former spouse, civil partner, or former civil partner by court order.
- the entire asset was sold for its cash value in a transaction on arm's length terms whether or not the parties were connected persons.
- the owner of the asset was formerly the owner of the asset only by virtue of a will or intestacy which has subsequently been varied by agreement between the parties, i.e., by a deed of family arrangement as explained further in the book.
- the asset is land or buildings which have been given and the donor and the person to whom it is given share the occupation of the land and either the donor pays all the running costs and capital expenses relating to the occupation of the property or an amount at least proportionate to his share of the ownership and use of

the property so that he cannot be said to be retaining any benefit from the arrangement.

- the gift does not take the asset out of the donor's taxable estate for inheritance tax purposes. e.g., a gift to a company in which the donor owns all the shares or the asset still counts as an asset of the donor for inheritance tax purposes under the gift with a reservation rules.

- any benefit is no more than incidental.

- the gift is an outright gift of money used to acquire land or another asset made seven years or more before the earliest date upon which the donor either occupied the land or had the use of the asset.

- the original gift was for the maintenance of the donor's family or within the small gift's exemption (£250 per donee) or within the annual gift allowance (£3000 in total.

- the donor is not resident in the UK.

- the asset which gives rise to the benefit is situated abroad and the donor does not have his domicile in the UK.

- the asset is a non-UK asset which the taxpayer ceased to own before he became domiciled in the UK.

- the aggregate benefits do not exceed more than £5000 in one year.

If the taxpayer so elects before 31st January after the end of the first tax year in which the pre-owned assets rule applies to him, he can choose to have the property in question treated as part of his estate for inheritance tax purposes as a gift with reservation of an interest rather than have the benefit taxed as an income. Whether it will be advantageous for a taxpayer to opt into inheritance tax by reason of the transaction being a gift with a reservation of a benefit instead of paying the pre-owned asset income tax charge will depend upon how long he has to live, the amount of the income tax charge and the rate at which his income is taxed.

If a taxpayer gives an asset away and pays a full commercial rent or hiring fee to use it, although doing so will save inheritance tax, it will not usually be an otherwise tax efficient tax efficient transaction because as far as income tax is concerned, the taxpayer will be paying the rent or hiring fee out of taxable income and the recipient of the gift will have to pay income tax on the rent. If the taxpayer's principal private residence is the subject of the transaction, the capital gains exemption for a principal private residence will be lost when the donee comes to sell the property unless during the period of the donor's benefit the donee also uses it as his principal private residence.

****

Chapter 5

The Various Inheritance Tax Reliefs Available

In this chapter we cover the following:

- Various relief's available when calculating IHT.
- Rates of relief.
- Businesses which do not attract relief.
- The minimum period of ownership.
- Shares and relief.
- Paying tax on business property.
- Agricultural property.
- Woodland relief.
- Death and military service.
- Deeds of family arrangement.

Certain circumstances, and property, attract inheritance tax relief. The main areas are listed below.

Taper relief

In the case of gifts made between three and seven years of death, tax is charged proportionately. The proportion will depend on how long the maker of the gift survives the making of the gift. This reduction is known as taper relief. If there's Inheritance Tax to pay, it's charged at 40% on gifts given in the 3 years before you die. Gifts made 3 to 7 years before your death are taxed on a sliding scale known as 'taper relief'. See table below.

Years between gifts and death	Tax paid
Less than 3	40%
3-4	32%
4-5	24%
5-6	16%
6-7	8%
More than 7	0%

See chapter 7 for more details on gifts and inheritance tax relief.

Business property relief

Business relief on certain types of business can be claimed if they qualify as a relevant business property and the transferor has owned them for a minimum period. Relief can be claimed for transfers made during a person's lifetime and on death and on chargeable occasions arising on relevant business property held on trust.

Types of business property on which relief can be claimed

A person can claim business relief on:

- a business or an interest in business (such as a partner in a partnership).
- unquoted shares. This includes shares which are traded in the unlisted securities market (USM shares) or the Alternative Investment market (AIM). Shares that are listed on a recognised overseas stock exchange are quoted for IHT purposes, even if they are also traded in the AIM or USM.
- A holding of shares or securities owned by the transferor, which are fully listed on a recognised stock exchange, which themselves or with other listed shares give control of a company.
- Land, buildings, plant or machinery owned by a partner of a controlling shareholder and used wholly or mainly in the business or the partnership or company immediately before the transfer. This applies only if the partnership interest or shareholding would itself, if transferred, qualify for business relief.
- Any land, buildings machinery or plant which was used wholly or mainly for the purpose of a business carried on by a transferor and was settled property in which the transferor was beneficially entitled to

an interest in possession and used in the transferor's business.

Rate of relief

If the asset qualifies for relief, the rate at which it is allowed is shown below. The relief is given by deducting the relevant percentage of the capital value of the asset. The below deals with transfers after 6th April 1996.

A business or an interest in a business   100%

A holding of shares in an unquoted company   100%

Control holding of shares in a quoted company   50%
(More than 50% of the voting rights)

 Land, buildings, plant or machinery used in a business of which the deceased was a partner at the date of death or used by a company controlled by the deceased. 50%

Land, buildings or machinery held in trust where the deceased had the right to benefit from the trust and the asset was used in a business carried on by the deceased. 50%

Business on which relief cannot be claimed

You can't claim Business Relief if the company:

- mainly deals with securities, stocks or shares, land, or buildings, or in making or holding investments.
- is a not-for-profit organisation.

- is being sold unless the sale is to a company that will carry on the business and the estate will be paid mainly in shares of that company.
- is being wound up unless this is part of a process to allow the business of the company to carry on.
- You can't claim Business Relief on an asset if it:
- also qualifies for Agricultural Relief
- wasn't used mainly for business in the 2 years before it was either passed on as a gift or as part of the will.
- isn't needed for future use in the business.
- If part of a non-qualifying asset is used in the business, that part might qualify for Business Relief.

Relief may be available for:

- the business of a market maker or discount house in the United Kingdom
- shares or securities in a company which is a holding company and the group is not wholly or mainly engaged in property, investment or dealing.

Calculating the value of relevant business property

If business relief is being deducted at 100% from the value of the deceased's business or interest in a business, the value of the business can include the value of the business as shown in the company's accounts. If you are not deducting business relief at 100% you will have to adjust the value taken from the company's accounts to ensure that you include the open market value of the business rather than the book value.

Individual assets in the business, such as land, buildings, stock, goodwill and machinery may be included at book value.

Excepted assets

Some assets are known as excepted and do not qualify for relief.

An asset is excepted if it is:

- not used wholly or mainly for the purposes of the business throughout the two years immediately before the transfer (or since its acquisition by the business if more recent)
- not required at the time of the transfer for identified future use for the purpose of the business, or
- used wholly or mainly for the personal benefit of the transferor, or a person connected with the transferor (e.g., spouse, child or relative).

Shares in a holding company

Special rules apply if the relevant business property is a controlling shareholding in a holding company. If the group includes any company whose own business falls outside the scope of the relief, business relief is only given on the value that would be appropriate if that company were not part of the group. In applying the rules for excepted assets, the group is treated as one concern.

The minimum period of ownership

The general rule is that property is not relevant business property (and so does not qualify for relief) unless it was owned as such by the transferor throughout the two years immediately before the transfer.

There are certain points to note:

- If the transferor becomes entitled to the property on the death of a spouse or civil partner, relief is available for any period during which the spouse or civil partner owned it.
- If the transferred property was acquired on an earlier transfer within the two-year period relief is available if:
  o The earlier transfer was eligible for business relief.
  o The earlier transfer was made to the current transferor or spouse or civil partner.
  o One of the transfers was made on death, and
  o The property, apart from the two-year rule, would qualify for relief.

o Relief is available when the transferred property replaces other relievable property.

o If the transferor inherits the property on death, the ownership is considered to run from the date of death.

Business relief and a gift of business property

Business relief is only given if, or to the extent that, the gifted property:

- was relevant business property at the time that the transfer was made.
- was owned by the transferee throughout the period between the gift and the death of the transferor, or the earlier death of the transferee, subject to special rules for replacement property (below).
- immediately before the transferor's death or the earlier death of the transferee, remains property eligible for relief as relevant business property.

It is available at the rate appropriate to the property at the time the gift occurred.

Part of a gift qualifying for relief

If, at the date of the transferor's death the conditions for relief are satisfied for only a part of the gifted property, a proportionate part of the value that was transferred is reduced. If the transferee dies before the transferor the conditions for relief must be satisfied at both the date of the gift and the time of the transferor's death.

Rules for replacement property

Where the original relevant business property was disposed of before the transferor's death and the proceeds were used to buy replacement property, the relief is not necessarily lost. In order to still qualify for relief:

- the whole of the sale proceeds must have been used to purchase the replacement property and
- both the sale and the purchase must have been arm's length transactions taking place within three years of each other.

The replacement property must also be of such a nature that, if it was transferred by the transferee immediately before the death of the transferor, it would, apart from the minimum period of ownership requirement, qualify for relief.

Generally, the property is treated as satisfying the two-year ownership test if:

(overleaf)

- it replaces other property (which may have replaced other property and so on)
- the transferor owned property in the chain for periods amounting to at least two years during the five years immediately before the transfer, and
- each item in the chain, which is taken into account for the two-year ownership period, would have been relevant business property (apart from the length of ownership) if the transfer of value had taken place immediately before the item was replaced.

Shares exchanged for other shares

Where shares are exchanged for other shares, the time of ownership of previous shares counts towards the two-year period. This can happen in a capital reorganisation or amalgamation.

Paying tax on business property

If inheritance tax is due and there is not 100% relief, business tax can be paid in instalments on:

- certain shares and securities. You may be able to pay tax in instalments if they gave the deceased control of the company at the time of the transfer or they are unquoted and either you can show that the tax attributable to their value could not be paid in one sum without undue hardship or at least 20% of the tax for which the same person is liable in the same capacity is attributable to assets that qualify for payment by instalments. In the case of unquoted shares only, their value exceeds £20,000 and the shares transferred represent at least 10% of the nominal value of the company's share capital or the ordinary share capital.

- the net value of a business or an interest in a business, including a profession or a vocation, carried on for gain (this does not include individual assets of a business, which are distinct from the business as a whole).

In certain cases, interest will be charged on instalments.

Agricultural property

You can pass on some agricultural property free of Inheritance Tax, either during your lifetime or as part of your will. Agricultural property that qualifies for Agricultural Relief is land or pasture that is used to grow crops or to rear animals intensively. It also includes:

- growing crops
- stud farms for breeding and rearing horses and grazing

- trees that are planted and harvested at least every 10 years (short-rotation coppice)
- land not currently being farmed under the Habitat Scheme
- land not currently being farmed under a crop rotation scheme
- the value of milk quota associated with the land
- some agricultural shares and securities
- farm buildings, farm cottages and farmhouses
- These do not qualify for Agricultural Relief:
- farm equipment and machinery
- derelict buildings
- harvested crops
- livestock
- property subject to a binding contract for sale

Location

A property may be owner occupied or let, but it must be part of a working farm in the:

- UK
- Channel Islands
- Isle of Man
- European Economic Area

Period of ownership or occupation

The property must have been owned and occupied for agricultural purposes immediately before its transfer for:

- 2 years if occupied by the owner, a company controlled by them, or their spouse or civil partner
- 7 years if occupied by someone else

Property received by transfer

When the person making the transfer originally inherited the property from someone other than a spouse or civil partner, the period of ownership is calculated from the date of that first death.

If the property was originally acquired through a transfer, the below conditions must also be met:

- the property must have qualified for Agricultural Relief at the date of the first transfer
- the property must have been occupied for agricultural purposes by the person making the later transfer or the personal representatives of the person the property originally came from
- the property should qualify for relief apart from the occupation and ownership tests
- one of the transfers must occur on death

Farmhouses and cottages

Buildings must be of a nature and size appropriate to the farming activity that is taking place. The property is valued as if it could only be used for agricultural purposes. Any value over and above this 'agricultural value', such as the market price of a country residence, does not qualify for Agricultural Relief. A cottage or farmhouse must be occupied by someone employed in farming or:

- a retired farm employee
- the spouse or civil partner of a deceased farm employee
- They must occupy the property as either a:
- tenant under a lease granted as part of their former employment contract
- protected tenant with statutory rights

Rates of Agricultural Relief

Agricultural Relief is due at 100% if:

- the person who owned the land farmed it themselves
- the land was used by someone else on a short-term grazing licence
- it was let on a tenancy that began on or after 1 September 1995

A property that was owned before 10 March 1981 can qualify for 100% relief if:

- it would have qualified under Schedule 8 Finance Act 1975 had it been transferred before that date
- the person who owned it had no possible right to vacant possession between that date and the date of the current transfer

Relief is due at a lower rate of 50% in any other case.

Mortgaged property

Deduct outstanding mortgages or any other secured liabilities on the property before calculating the Agricultural Relief.

Agricultural shares and securities

Some company shares and securities are eligible for Agricultural Relief if their value:

- gave the deceased control of the company at the time of death
- comes from agricultural property that forms part of the company's assets

Gifts of agricultural property

If a gift (or portion of a gift) qualified for Agricultural Relief at the time it was made, it will still qualify if it:

- has been held by the person who received it until their own death or that of the person who gave the gift
- is agricultural property that has been occupied for agricultural purposes since the gift was made

If the person receiving the gift dies before the person who gave the gift, conditions for relief have to be met both on the date that the gift is given and at the time of their death.

If the person receiving a gift sells it, before the death of the person giving the gift, to a company in exchange for shares in that company then those shares are treated as the original property.

Any additional shares received as a result of a re-organisation or take-over-bid are treated as part of the original gift.

Replacement agricultural property

If agricultural property that qualified for Agricultural Relief is replaced by other agricultural property that also qualifies for relief (apart from the minimum period of ownership requirement) then all the following conditions must be met if the original property was gifted:

- all of the sale proceeds must be used to purchase the replacement property

- the sale and purchase must be an 'arms length transaction' in which the buyers and sellers act independently and have no relationship to each other.
- the sale and purchase must take place within 3 years of each other.

The original and the replacement property combined must satisfy the conditions shown under 'Gifts of agricultural property'. If the agricultural property was in a person's estate when they died and it had replaced other agricultural property it can still qualify for Agricultural Relief if the original and replacement property:

- has been occupied by the owner, for the purposes of agriculture, for a total period of at least 2 years during the 5 years immediately before the death
- was owned and occupied (either by the owner or by someone else) for the purposes of agriculture for at least 7 years during the 10 years immediately before the death.

Relief is limited to what would have been available before the replacement. If the property was sold at less than the market value, relief is limited by the proportion that was given as a gift.

Example

John sells a field on his farm worth £2,000 to his son David on the next-door farm for £500. This means that he is giving David a gift of 75% of the value of the field = £1,500.

David sells the field a year later and uses the £2,000 from the sale to buy another field for £2,000.

John dies 3 years after the sale.

When IHT is calculated the original market value (£2,000) of the field, less the £500 paid (the value that was transferred), rather than the current market value of the field (£2,500) is included as a gift made by John and is eligible for Agricultural Relief.

Business relief

You cannot claim Business Relief on the value of an asset that you have already claimed Agricultural Relief on. However, a farming business may find that Business Relief is available on the value of an asset not fully covered by Agricultural Relief if the conditions are met.

Woodland relief

IHT is potentially charged at 40% on the woodland of a deceased owner, though that only applies if the deceased person had assets of more than £325,000. There is also no IHT charged where assets are transferred to a spouse. This

40% tax is on the market value of the woodland so one can see that without various exemptions it would be hard to keep woodland in the family and hard to keep rural estates together. For woodland owners IHT can be legitimately avoided, reduced or deferred in three different ways.

The main way to avoid paying IHT is to make sure that the woodland qualifies as a business asset which formally means you would be using the Inheritance Tax Act of 1984 (IHTA) where you can get 100% relief from this tax if the woodland is both commercially managed (in other words it has been run as a business) and has been owned for at least 2 years. As the woodland owner you will need to show that the woodland has been managed with a view to generating timber income or capital gain from the increase in the value of the timber. The sorts of thing that HMRC look for are the existence of a management plan where the principal objective is timber production, evidence that the plan has been actioned and updated, and proof of budgets and financial records. Typically, a Forestry-Commission-approved Woodland Management Plan will have been drawn up that also enables an owner to obtain grants which further help to prove "commerciality". Of course, HMRC will look at the relief claim after death and it is up to the inheritor/beneficiary to provide the evidence on which HMRC can make a decision. However, it is quite possible that a woodland owner dies without having shown serious business intent, but all is not lost – there are two other routes to reduce or defer IHT.

The second route is the use of Agricultural Property Relief which essentially means that you can show that the woodland was part of an agricultural holding, perhaps used as a shelter belt. But this use must be shown to be occupied along with agricultural land or pasture and also used in conjunction with it (ancillary use), so it is fairly unlikely that many owners of small woods – living some distance away from their woodlands – will be able to use this relief.

However, there is a third IHT relief which many woodlands will be able to use, called "Woodland Relief". This allows IHT to be deferred on the value of the growing timber until such time as that timber is felled and sold, which in practice may be an almost indefinite period.

Quick succession relief

Quick succession relief is given when someone dies and his/her estate has been increased by a taxable disposition in his favour within the previous five years. The idea is to reduce the tax payable on the second transfer of assets within the five years. It is not essential for the property given by the first disposition to have been retained by the person concerned until the time of the second disposition.

The relief operates by reducing the tax payable on the second occasion by a sum equal to a percentage of the tax paid on the first occasion in respect of the increase in value of the second estate by the asset concerned. The increase is calculated on the basis of the net increase after deduction of tax and allowing for reliefs such as business relief but without any deduction for the expenses of administering the estate. It is a tax credit and it is the tax payable that is reduced, not the value of the asset. The percentage depends on how long has elapsed between the two dispositions:

- if less than one year has elapsed the percentage is 100%
- between one and two years 80%
- two and three years 60%
- between three and four years 40%
- between four and five years 20%

When does Quick Succession Relief not apply?

QSR does not apply if:

- the transfer to the deceased was exempt
- the transfer to the deceased was chargeable but no IHT was paid as it was below the IHT thresholds
- the transfer to the deceased was made more than five years before the deceased's death
- no IHT is payable on the deceased's death.

If QSR is available but is not used as the estate is left to a surviving spouse or civil partner, the unused QSR is not transferable.

How to calculate Quick Succession Relief
The calculation for QSR is as follows.

- The amount of increase in the deceased's estate is divided by the value of the earlier chargeable transfer
- This amount is then multiplied by the tax due on the earlier chargeable transfer
- This amount is then multiplied by the appropriate percentage

Example
I have tried to give a simple example which hopefully will highlight how you work out QSR.

Peter dies in November 2020. His estate is worth £700,000. Peter inherited his mother's estate after her death in August 2018. Her estate was £450,000 and IHT of £50,000 was due on his mother's death. Peter also inherited on his wife's death in April 2017 when she divided her estate equally between Peter and her children. IHT of £20,000 was due on his wife's death.

Peter's estate of £700,000 passes to his friend Gwen. IHT is due on his death and as he inherited from transfers within the past 5 years QSR relief can be considered. QSR relief will be due on the inheritance from his mother under the 60% relief but not from his wife as the transfer to Peter was exempt from IHT.

QSR available on his death would be calculated as follows. All decimals are rounded to two decimal points:

The amount of increase in the deceased's estate by the previous transfer £450,000 – £50,000 = £400,000

Divided by earlier chargeable transfer (£450,000) = 0.89

Multiplied by tax due on earlier transfer (£50,000) = £44,444.44

Multiplied by 60% = £26,666.67.

His IHT bill would be calculated as follows:

- £700,000 – £325,000 (nil rate band) = £375,000
- Multiplied by 40% = £150,000
- Minus the QSR (£26,666.67) = £123,333.33

Relief for Heritage assets

Limited conditional relief is given in respect of land, buildings and objects which appear to the Treasury of being of outstanding importance from the point of view of national heritage. The relief is dependent on specified obligations to preserve the asset and allow public access to it being undertaken by the donor.

Death and military service

If a serving or former member of the Armed Forces dies from (or death can be shown to have been hastened by) an injury sustained or disease contracted on active service against the enemy or other service of a warlike nature (such as operations against hostile forces in peace time or anti-terrorist operations), a complete exemption from inheritance tax can be granted on their estate under the provisions of s154 of the Inheritance Tax Act. Likewise, whilst the total exemption is not transferable to a spouse's estate, the granting of an exemption on the veteran's estate will double the personal tax threshold (to £650,000) used to assess any Inheritance Tax liability on the spouse's estate when they die.

Each application for an exemption is considered on its merits, after the death of the veteran concerned and requires the MoD to be given access to the veteran's full medical records. Neither war time service in the armed forces, or receipt of a war pension, is a guarantee exemption will be granted.

Anyone wishing to apply for an exemption under s154, on a veteran's estate, or requiring further information, should contact Veterans UK. Contact the agency on www.veterans-uk.info or on 0808 1914 2 18.

Relief for land and assets sold within a short time of death

It is sometimes possible to adjust for inheritance tax purposes the value attributed to any stock exchange securities (other than those quoted on the AIM market), shares in common investment funds, unit trusts, and land and buildings which are sold in the course of administration of the estate at a loss compared with their value as declared in the probate papers, to reflect the sale price rather than the value at the date of death.

To obtain an agreement by HMRC to a revaluation in the case of stock exchange securities, shares in common investment funds and unit trusts they must have been sold within twelve months of the date of the death.

Deeds of Family Arrangement

It is possible for the beneficiaries of a will, or those who inherit a share of an estate upon intestacy, to vary the terms of the will or the inheritance on intestacy by agreement after the death. This is done by a voluntary agreement contained in a document known as a Deed of family Arrangement or by a deed of disclaimer. Similarly, the personal representatives of a beneficiary who survives his benefactor and then dies can vary the inheritance if they have the consent of those who benefit under his will or upon his intestacy If this special provision was not made then any such variation would constitute a taxable disposition.

Basically, under the Inheritance Tax Act if a variation is made within two years of the death and certain other conditions are complied with, the transfer shall not be considered a transfer of value and the variation is viewed as if it had been made by the deceased. Distributions made within two years of the testator's death from discretionary trusts created by his will are also considered to have been made by the deceased's will.

Double taxation relief

If an asset which is situated overseas is subject to a tax similar to inheritance tax in a foreign country and also to inheritance tax in the UK, relief will be given as a credit against UK tax payable in respect of the overseas asset.

The relief given is the lower of the foreign tax which has been paid in respect of the asset and the UK tax which would otherwise be payable in respect of the asset, the UK tax being calculated at the average percentage rate payable in respect of the estate.

Limiting the set-off of debts

Following the introduction of the Finance Act 2013, as amended, new rules were brought into play concerning set-off of debts. Where a non-domiciled individual (or the trustees of his trust) borrows from a bank secured on a UK property and deposit the borrowed funds on a back to back basis (or use them for investing offshore) the debt will not be allowable on the individual's death. This will increase the inheritance taxable estate. Nor will the debt be allowable in calculating inheritance tax charges in the trust.

Entrepreneurs who borrow to invest in their business but secure the borrowing on other assets will have the borrowing deducted from the business assets leaving their family with a bigger inheritance tax bill. This also applies where the borrowings are used in relation to agricultural property and woodlands.

Debts which are not repaid after an individual's death, may also be disallowed. The time limit for repayment is not specified but the debt must be discharged "after death, out of the estate" which suggests that it must be repaid during administration of the estate if it is to be allowable.

Debts are not disallowed where there is a "real commercial reason" for the debt not being repaid. This will be the case where there is an arm's length borrowing or, if the borrowing is from someone other than a third party, a third party in the same circumstances would not require the debt to be paid.

In addition, the liability must not be left unpaid as part of "arrangements where the main purpose, or one of the main purposes, is to secure a tax advantage".

The definitions of "arrangements" and "tax advantage" are very wide. A tax advantage includes a delay in a charge to tax or even the avoidance of a possible assessment or determination in respect of tax as well as obtaining a relief or repayment or reduction in the tax. "Tax" is expressly defined to include income tax and capital gains tax.

Before the disguised remuneration provisions were introduced, it was common for Employee Benefit Trusts (EBTs) to make loans to beneficiaries which were left outstanding indefinitely and might be waived after the individual's death. These sorts of loans will, if not repaid by the estate after the ex-employee's death, be disallowed in calculating inheritance tax. This creates a catch-22 situation. The disguised remuneration rules provide that if the loan is waived after death, the individual's estate or heirs will be subject to an income tax charge.

But if the loan remains outstanding, there is no deduction from the estate, potentially increasing the inheritance tax due.

****

Chapter 6

Different Trusts and Inheritance Tax

In this chapter we will cover the following:

- Definition of a trust
- Property
- Beneficiaries
- Creation of a trust
- Trustees
- Different types of trusts
- Taxation of trusts
- Inheritance tax and trusts
- Trusts and capital gains tax

Trusts can be a very effective tool indeed when planning inheritance tax and it is essential to know the basics of trusts and how they can be utilised.

Definition of a trust

Put simply, a trust is an obligation binding a person, or persons, which can be an individual or company, (a trust can have up to four trustees) to deal with 'property' in a particular way, for the benefit of one or more beneficiaries.

Trustees

Trustees are the legal owners of the trust property. They are legally bound to look after the property of the trust in a particular way and for a particular purpose. Trustees administer the trust and in certain circumstances make decisions about how the property in the trust is to be used. Trustees can change, but there must be a minimum of one trustee.

Property

The property of a trust can include:

- Money
- Investments
- Land or buildings
- Other assets

The cash and investments held in a trust are also called the 'capital' or 'fund' of the trust. The capital or fund may produce income and the land or buildings may produce income. The way income is taxed will depend on the nature or type of the trust.

The beneficiary of the trust

A beneficiary is anyone who benefits from the property held in the trust. There can be any number of beneficiaries, such as a whole family or class of people and each can benefit from the trust in a different way. Beneficiaries can benefit from:

- Income only
- Capital only
- Both the income and capital

The Settlor

A settler is anyone who has put property into a trust. The trust may be created by an express statement of the settlor (an express trust) or by implication from his conduct or presumed intention (an implied or resulting trust) or imposed by law to achieve fairness in a certain situation (constructive trust). This section is concerned with express trusts. Property is normally put into a trust when it is created but it can be added at a later time.

Creating a trust

Normally, a trust is created by deed. Usually, a settlor will ask a professional advisor to draw up a trust deed, which in turn sets out the terms of the trust. A trust can be created under the terms of a will when someone leaves instructions that when he or she dies all or some of the estate is placed in trust. A trust can also occur if someone dies without leaving a will Sometimes a court will create a trust, for example when deciding how to deal with property for the benefit of children or for someone who is incapacitated in some way.

The responsibilities of a trustee

The trustee will have to make provision for any tax owed. The responsibility of a trustee will depend very much on the type of trust (see below for explanation of the different trusts). The settlor may have given instructions that trustees carry out certain functions and the law may impose other duties.

For tax purposes the trustee is responsible for:

- Notifying the HMRC that income tax is due, within six months of the end of the tax year for which it is due
- Keeping records of the income and capital gains of the trust
- Completing and sending back tax returns relating to the trust
- Paying any tax due
- Supplying certificates or vouchers to the beneficiaries to show how much income they have received from the trust in the tax year and how

much tax the trustees have deducted. Professional advisors may be appointed but it is ultimately the trustee's responsibility.

As a trustee, if a trust is wound up HMRC should be notified and final tax returns completed. Provisions will have to be made for any tax owed.

The different sorts of trust

Although there are a number of different sorts of trust, they will usually fall into one of the below categories:

- Bare trusts
- Interest in possession trusts
- Discretionary trusts
- Accumulation trusts
- Mixed trusts
- Settlor-interested trusts
- non-resident trusts

The bare trust

Assets in a bare trust are held in the name of a trustee. However, the beneficiary has the right to all of the capital and income of the trust at any time if they're 18 or over (in England and Wales), or 16 or over (in Scotland). This means the assets set aside by the settlor will always go directly to the intended beneficiary. Bare trusts are often used to pass assets to young people - the trustees look after them until the beneficiary is old enough.

The (limited) interest in possession trust

This type of trust exists when a beneficiary, known in this case as an 'income beneficiary' has a current legal right to the income from the trust as it arises. The trustees must pass over all the income received, less any trustees' expenses and taxes, to the beneficiary. A beneficiary who is entitled to the income of the trust for life is known as a life tenant, or as having a life interest. The income beneficiary need not, and often does not, have any rights over the capital of such a trust. Normally, the capital will pass over to a different beneficiary(s) at a specific time in the future or after a specific event. Depending on o the terms of the trust, the trustees might have the power to pay capital to a beneficiary even though the beneficiary only has the right to receive income. A beneficiary who is entitled to the trust capital is known as the 'remainderman', or the 'capital beneficiary'.

Uses for interest in possession trusts

Interest in possession trusts are very useful in the case of second or subsequent marriages if a taxpayer wishes his assets to benefit his spouse after his death but to ensure that they are inherited by his/her children and no one else after his/her death.

Interest in possession trusts are also useful to provide for the maintenance of individual children in a family until they are capable of providing for themselves.

The discretionary trust

Trustees of a discretionary trust generally have discretion about how to use the income of the trust. They may be required to use the income for the benefit f any specific beneficiaries, but can also decide:

- How much is paid
- To which beneficiary or class of beneficiaries payments are made
- How often payments are made
- What (if any) conditions to impose on the beneficiaries

The trustees may, or may not, be allowed to 'accumulate' income within the trust for as long as the law allows rather than pass it to the beneficiaries. Income that has been accumulated becomes part of the assets of the trust.

Discretionary trusts are sometimes set up to put assets aside for:

- a future need, like a grandchild who may need more financial help than other beneficiaries at some point in their life
- beneficiaries who are not capable or responsible enough to deal with money themselves.

Bereaved Minor Trusts and 18 to 25 trusts

A Will making a gift to children conditional on their attaining a particular age will create either a Bereaved Minor Trust or an 18 – 25 Trust.

Bereaved Minor Trusts

Where a Will sets up a trust for children of the deceased, who will inherit subject to the condition that they attain the age of 18, this will normally create a 'Bereaved Minor Trust'. A Bereaved Minor Trust must be distinguished from a gift in a Will made without any age restriction, where the beneficiary happens to be a child, or a gift left absolutely to a child but directed to be payable when they are older. These will create a Bare Trust, in which the gifts given belong to the child from the start. Due to a change in the law, Bereaved Minor Trusts can now only be created by parents for their own children or stepchildren. Any money left to grandchildren, nephews and nieces or other minor beneficiaries will create either a Bare Trust or a Relevant Property Trust.

From 22 March 2006, an 'age 18 to 25 trust' is a discretionary trust set up under the will or intestacy of a deceased parent or stepparent, where the property is held on trust for the benefit of someone aged over 18 and under 25. Accumulation and maintenance trusts set up before 22 March 2006 which provide for the beneficiaries to become absolutely entitled to the trust fund on or before the age of 25 will become age 18 to 25 trust if, before 6 April 2008, they rewrite the trust to comply with the new rules. The property in an 18 to 25 trust is subject to age18 to 25 exit charges when property leaves the trust on or before the beneficiary's twenty-fifth birthday.

Uses of discretionary trusts

The principal advantage of a discretionary trust is that no inheritance tax is payable upon the death of a potential beneficiary because no beneficiary has a right to a defined interest in the trust assets or the income that they produce until the trustees have exercised their discretion in his favour. A further benefit is that of flexibility. Within the wide boundaries set out in a trust deed a discretionary trust permits the trustees to use the trust fund in any way that they consider to be most appropriate at the time.

Discretionary trusts are frequently used to provide for people whose financial needs are likely to vary at different times in the future or to protect the trust fund from creditors if one of the potential beneficiaries is a spendthrift or engaged in risky business ventures that could end in bankruptcy.

Trust for Vulnerable Beneficiaries

Some trusts for disabled people or children get special tax treatment. These are called 'trusts for vulnerable beneficiaries'.

Who qualifies as a vulnerable beneficiary

A vulnerable beneficiary is either someone under 18 whose parent has died or a disabled person who is eligible for any of the following benefits (even if they do not receive them):

- Attendance Allowance (either the care component at the middle or highest rate, or the mobility component at the highest rate)
- Personal Independence Allowance
- an increased disablement pension
- Constant Attendance Allowance
- Armed Forces Independence Payment

A vulnerable beneficiary can also be someone who is unable to manage their own affairs because of a mental health condition - check with a medical professional that it's covered by the Mental Health Acts.

Accumulation trusts

This is where the trustees can accumulate income within the trust and add it to the trust's capital. They may also be able to pay income out, as with discretionary trusts.

Mixed trust

A mixed trust is a mixture of more than one type of trust, for example an interest in possession trust and a discretionary trust, or an interest in possession trust and an accumulation and maintenance trust.

Settlor-interested trust

There are special tax rules in which the settlor 'retains an interest' in the trust for example where the settlor receives an income from the trust. However, this type of trust will not be covered further because of its highly specialised nature.

Non-resident trusts and special trusts

Again, the rules for these trusts are too complicated and would need a professional advisor to elaborate these rules. Examples of such trusts include:

- Trusts where some or all of the trustees are not UK residents

- Trusts that are not created or are not administered under UK law
- Various special types of UK trust such as charities, pension funds, unit trusts and trusts for employee share schemes.

The taxation of trusts

The tax regime covers the different types of trusts in relation to capital gains tax, income tax and also inheritance tax. In the first section we deal with income tax and capital gains tax and then finally inheritance tax. Depending on the type of trust, when income and capital gains tax arise in a trust, tax might be charged on:

- The trustees
- The beneficiaries
- The settlor

Taxation of trusts generally

A trust, for UK tax purposes, is a separate legal entity and the trustees of a trust are considered as a body distinct from the individuals who compose it.

Taxation of trusts must be considered in respect of inheritance tax, capital gains tax and income tax at three stages of its existence: when assets are transferred into the trust, during the continuance of the trust and when assets are transferred out of the trust, including when the trust terminates.

Taxation of bare trusts

Bare trusts are created for tax purposes as if the beneficiary holds the trust property in his or her own name. Income tax and capital gains tax are charged on the beneficiary. The beneficiary must declare any income and capital gains on their personal tax return. Although trustees can pay income tax on behalf of a beneficiary, it is the beneficiary who is chargeable to tax.

Interest in possession trusts and tax

The trustees of this type of trust are normally chargeable to income tax on income received.

- UK dividend income is chargeable at the starting rate for dividends (currently 8% 2023/2024) and the tax credit attached to the net dividend meets the trustee's liability.
- All other income @20%

Sometimes the trustees 'mandate' income to the beneficiary. This means it goes to them directly instead of being passed through the trustees. If this happens, the beneficiary needs to include this on their Self Assessment tax return and pay tax on it. The beneficiaries are entitled to the income from the trust after tax and expenses and are taxed on this in the normal way. They are entitled to credit for tax paid by the trustees or deducted at source.

If beneficiaries are starting rate taxpayers or non-taxpayers, they will be able to claim some or all of the tax paid, though tax credits on dividends cannot be claimed. If they are liable at higher rates then further tax will be due.

Accumulation and Discretionary trusts and tax-Income Tax

Trustees are responsible for declaring and paying Income Tax on income received by the trust. They do this on form SA900 Trust and Estate Tax Return each year.

In both discretionary trusts and accumulation trusts, income is taxed at the special trust rates, apart from the first £1,000 of trust income, which is known as the 'standard rate band'. Income that falls within the standard rate band is taxed at lower rates, depending on the nature of the income - as shown in the tables below. However, if the person who put the assets into the trust (the settlor) has more than one trust, the £1,000 standard rate band is divided by the number of trusts they have.

If the settlor has more than five trusts, the standard rate band is £200 for each trust. The tax rates are as follows (2023/24):

Trust income up to £1,000

Type of Income	Tax rate
Dividend type income	8%
All other income	20%

Trust income over £1,000

Type of income	Tax rate
Dividend type income	**39.35%**
All other income	45%

Dividends

Trustees do not qualify for the dividend allowance. This means trustees pay tax on all dividends depending on the tax band they fall within.

Mixed trusts

Mixed trusts will be taxed under the rules for that type of trust, e.g., the part of a trust that is an interest in possession will be taxed as such and so on.

Payment of tax

Trustees may need to pay tax for any one year in three instalments, as follows:

- a payment on account on 31st January in the tax year

- another payment on account on 31st July after the end of the tax year, and
- a final payment on the following 31st January if further tax is due.

For full details of current tax rates go to: www.gov.uk/trusts-taxes/trusts-and-income-tax

Trusts and Inheritance Tax

Inheritance Tax may have to be paid on a person's estate (their money and possessions) when they die. Inheritance Tax is due at 40% on anything above the threshold – but there's a reduced rate of 36% if the person's will leaves more than 10% of their estate to charity. Inheritance Tax can also apply when you're alive if you transfer some of your estate into a trust.

When Inheritance Tax is due

The main situations when Inheritance Tax is due are:

- When assets are transferred into trust
- When a trust reaches a 10-yearly anniversary of when it was set up (there are 10-yearly Inheritance Tax charge)
- When assets are transferred out of a trust (known as 'exit charges') or the trust ends
- When someone dies and a trust is involved when sorting out their estate

What you pay Inheritance Tax on

You pay Inheritance Tax on 'relevant property' – assets like money, shares, houses, or land. This includes the assets in most trusts. There are some occasions where you may not have to pay Inheritance Tax – for example where the trust contains excluded property.

Special rules

Some types of trust are treated differently for Inheritance Tax purposes.

Bare trusts

As discussed, these are where the assets in a trust are held in the name of a trustee but go directly to the beneficiary, who has a right to both the assets and income of the trust. Transfers into a bare trust may also be exempt from Inheritance Tax, as long as the person making the transfer survives for 7 years after making the transfer.

Interest in possession trust

These are trusts where the beneficiary is entitled to trust income as it's produced – this is called their 'interest in possession'. On assets transferred into this type of trust before 22 March 2006, there's no Inheritance Tax to pay. On assets transferred on or after 22 March 2006, the 10-yearly Inheritance Tax charges may be due.

From 5 October 2008:

Beneficiaries of an interest in possession trust cannot pass their interest on as a transitional serial interest. If an interest is transferred after this date there may be a charge of 20% and a 10-yearly Inheritance Tax charge will be payable unless it's a disabled trust. If you inherit an interest in possession trust from someone who has died, there's no Inheritance Tax at the 10-yearly anniversary, instead, 40% tax will be due when you die.

If the trust is set up by a will

Someone might ask that some or all of their assets are put into a trust. This is called a 'will trust'. The personal representative of the deceased person must make sure that the trust is properly set up with all taxes paid, and the trustees make sure that Inheritance Tax is paid on any future charges.

If the deceased transferred assets into a trust before they died

If you're valuing the estate of someone who has died, you'll need to find out whether they made any transfers in the 7 years before they died. If they did, and they paid 20% Inheritance Tax, you'll need to pay an extra 20% from the estate. Even if no Inheritance Tax was due on the transfer, you still have to add its value to the person's estate when you're valuing it for Inheritance Tax purposes.

Trust for bereaved minors

A bereaved minor is a person under 18 who has lost at least one parent or stepparent. Where a trust is set up for a bereaved minor, there are no Inheritance Tax charges if:

- The assets in the trust are set aside just for bereaved minors.
- They become fully entitled to the assets by the age of 18.
- A trust for a bereaved young person can also be set up as an 18 to 25 trust – the 10-yearly charges do not apply. However, the main differences are:
- The beneficiary must become fully entitled to the assets in the trust by the age of 25 when the beneficiary is aged between 18 and 25. Inheritance Tax exit charges may apply.

Trust for disabled beneficiaries

There's no 10-yearly charge or exit charge on this type of trust as long as the asset stays in the trust and remains the 'interest' of the beneficiary. You also do not have to pay Inheritance Tax on the transfer of assets into a trust for a disabled person as long as the person making the transfer survives for 7 years after making the transfer.

Paying Inheritance Tax

You pay Inheritance Tax using form IHT100. If you're valuing the estate of someone who's died, you may have to value other assets apart from trust to see if Inheritance Tax is due.

Beneficiaries – paying and reclaiming tax on a trust

If you're a trust beneficiary there are different rules depending on the type of trust. You might have to pay tax through Self Assessment or you might be entitled to a tax refund. If you do not usually send a tax return and need to, you must register for Self Assessment by 5 October following the tax year you had the income.

Bare trusts

If you're the beneficiary of a bare trust you are responsible for declaring and paying tax on its income. Do this on a Self Assessment tax return. If you do not usually send a tax return and need to, you must register for Self Assessment by 5 October following the tax year you had the income.

Interest in possession trusts

If you're the beneficiary of this type of trust, you're entitled to its income ((after expenses) as it arises. If you ask for a statement, the trustee must tell you:

- The different sources of income.
- How much income you've been given.
- How much tax has been paid on the income.

You'll usually get income sent through the trustees, but they might pass it to you directly without paying tax first. If this happens you need to include it on your Self Assessment by 5 October the year after you were given the income.

If you're a basic rate taxpayer

You will not owe any extra tax. You'll only need to complete a Self-Assessment tax return if the income you receive from an interest in possession trust takes your total annual income into the higher rate income Tax band.

If you're a higher rate taxpayer

You'll have to pay extra tax on the difference between what tax the trustees have paid and what you, as a higher rate taxpayer, are liable for. This will be calculated when you do your Self Assessment.

How to reclaim tax

You can reclaim tax paid on:

- dividends (if you're entitled to dividend allowance)

- savings interest (if you're entitled to personal savings allowance)
- trade and property income (if you're entitled to trading allowance or property allowance)

The allowance amount will be reduced if it's already been used against some income. The allowance you have left is called the 'available allowance'.

If the amount of income you receive is less than or equal to the available allowance, you can reclaim all of the tax paid.

If the amount of income you receive is more than the available allowance, you can only claim the tax paid on the available allowance.

Accumulation or discretionary trusts

With these trusts all income received by beneficiaries is treated as though it has already been taxed at 45%. If you're an additional rate taxpayer there will be no more tax to pay.

You may be able to claim tax back on trust income you've received if any of the following apply:

- you're a non-taxpayer.
- you pay tax at the basic rate of 20%.
- you pay tax at the higher rate of 40%

You can reclaim the tax paid using form R40. If you complete a tax return, you can claim through Self Assessment.

Settlor-interested discretionary trusts

If a settlor-interested trust is a discretionary trust, payments made to the settlor's spouse or civil partner are treated as though they've already been taxed at 45%. There's no more tax to pay. However, unlike payments made from other types of trusts, the tax credit cannot be claimed back.

Non-resident trusts

This is a trust where the trustees are not resident in the UK for tax purposes. The tax rules for this type of trust are very complicated.

If a pension scheme pays into a trust

When a pension scheme pays a taxable lump sum into a trust after the pension holder dies, the payment is taxed at 45%, If you're a beneficiary and receive a payment funded by this lump sum, you'll also be taxed. You can claim back tax paid on the original lump sum – do this on your Self Assessment tax return if you complete one or using form R40. The trust will tell you the amount you need to report –

this will normally be more than the amount you actually receive.

Trustees – tax responsibilities

As the trustee, you're responsible for reporting and paying tax on behalf of the trust. If there are 2 or more trustees, nominate one as the 'principal acting trustee' to manage its tax. The other trustees are still accountable and can be charged tax interest if the trust does not pay.

Registering your trust

You need to register your trust with HM Revenue and Customs (HMRC) if it pays or owes any of the following:

- Capital Gains tax.
- Income Tax.
- Inheritance Tax.

You can only register one trust at a time. There's a different process if you need to register an estate for someone who's died.

Registration deadline for new trust

Register by 5 October in the tax year after the trust starts to pay any of the following for the first time:

- Capital Gains Tax
- Capital Gains Tax with Inheritance Tax
- Income Tax

Registration deadline for existing trusts

Register by 31 January for the previous tax year if your trust paid either:

- Capital Gains Tax
- Income Tax

Sending tax returns

You must report the trust's income and gains in a trust and estate Self Assessment tax return after the end of each tax year. You can either:

- Buy software to send it electronically by 31 January.
- Fill in paper form SA900 and post it to HMRC by 31 October (3 months earlier).

After you've sent your return, HMRC will tell you how much you owe. You'll need to pay your Self Assessment bill by the deadline. You'll need to collect and keep records (for example bank statements) to complete your tax return.

Telling beneficiaries about tax and income

You must give the beneficiary a statement with the amount of income and tax paid by the trust if they ask. You can use form R185 (trust) to do this. There's a different form if you need to provide a statement to a settlor who retains an interest. If there's more than one beneficiary, you must give each of them this information relative to the amount they receive.

Death benefit payments from a pension scheme

You must give the beneficiary extra information if both the following apply:

- You make a payment funded by a taxable lump sum from a pension scheme.
- The pension holder has died. Use form R185 (LSDB) if you're a trustee. There's a different form if you're a pension administrator. You must tell the beneficiary within 30 days.

Other responsibilities

- You may have to report other things to HMRC. You need to:
- use the online service to tell HMRC if there are any changes to the Trust.
- fill in form IHT 100when the trust needs to pay Inheritance Tax .

Your other responsibilities as a trustee depend on the type of trust and any instructions from the person who set up the trust in the trust deed.

Trusts and capital gains tax

Capital Gains Tax is a tax on the profit ('gain') when something (an 'asset') that's increased in value is taken out of or put into a trust.

When Capital Gains Tax might be payable

If assets are put into a trust tax is paid by either the person:

- selling the asset to the trust
- transferring the asset (the 'settlor')

If assets are taken out of a trust the trustees usually must pay the tax if they sell or transfer assets on behalf of the beneficiary. There's no tax to pay in bare trusts if the assets are transferred to the beneficiary.

Sometimes an asset might be transferred to someone else but Capital Gains Tax is not payable. This happens when someone dies and an 'interest in possession' ends.

A beneficiary gets some or all of the assets in a trust

Sometimes the beneficiary of a trust becomes 'absolutely entitled' and can tell the trustees what to do with the assets, for example when they reach a certain age. In this case, the trustees pay Capital Gains Tax based on the assets' market value when the beneficiary became entitled to them.

Working out total gains

Trustees need to work out the total taxable gain to know if they have to pay Capital Gains Tax.

Allowable costs

Trustees can deduct costs to reduce gains, including:

- the cost of the property (including any administration fees)
- professional fees, for example for a solicitor or stockbroker
- the cost of improving property or land to increase its value, for example building a conservatory (but not repairs or regular maintenance)

Tax reliefs

Trustees might be able to reduce or delay the amount of tax the trust pays if gains are eligible for tax relief.

Relief	Description
Private Residence Relief	Trustees pay no capital gains tax when they sell a property the trust owns. It must be the main residence for someone to live there under the rules of the trust.

Entrepreneurs Relief	Trustees pay 10% Capital Gains Tax on qualifying gains if they sell assets used in a beneficiary's business, which has now ended. They may also get relief when they sell shares in a company where the beneficiary had at least 5% of shares and voting rights.
Hold-Over Relief	Trustees pay no tax if they transfer assets to beneficiaries (or other trustees in some cases). The recipient pays tax when they sell or dispose of the assets unless they also claim relief.

Tax-free allowance

Trustees only have to pay Capital Gains Tax if the total taxable gain is above the trust's tax-free allowance (called the Annual Exempt Amount). The tax-free allowance for trusts is (2023/24):

- £3,000
- £6,000 if the beneficiary is vulnerable - a disabled person or a child whose parent has died.

If there's more than one beneficiary, the higher allowance may apply even if only one of them is vulnerable.

The tax-free allowance may be reduced if the trust's settlor has set up more than one trust ('settlement') since 6 June 1978.

Report gains to HMRC

If you're the trustee, report any gains as part of your Trust and Estate Tax Return. If you're the beneficiary, you need to report and pay through a Self Assessment tax return. Trustees must report and pay any tax due on UK residential property using a Capital Gains Tax on UK property account.

They must do this within:
- 60 days of selling the property if the completion date was on or after 27 October 2021
- 30 days of selling the property if the completion date was between 6 April 2020 and 26 October 2021

Trustees must report the sale or transfer of other assets in a trust and estate Self Assessment tax return.

Download and fill in a Trust and Estate Tax Capital Gains form (SA905) if you're a trustee sending a tax return by post.

****

Chapter 7

Inheritance Tax-Reducing the Bill

In this chapter we will cover the following:
- Gifts and exemptions
- Gifts with reservation of benefits
- Life assurance
- The family home
- Wills and deeds of variation
- Charity

As we have seen throughout the book, there are various ways of handling inheritance tax in order to reduce the actual burden on beneficiaries and executors of the estate. This chapter draws the various strands together and reminds you what can be done during your lifetime to reduce your inheritance tax bill.

As we have also seen, those above the nil-rate band of inheritance tax, currently £325,000 in 2023/2024 will be liable to pay 40% of the value of the estate above the band. We need to refresh ourselves on what can be done to ensure that the actual value of the estate is kept to a minimum. First, we should look at gifts and exemptions.

Gifts and exemptions

Generally speaking, gifts made during a person's lifetime are not chargeable to IHT when made but constitute a Potentially Exempt Transfer. Unless you have reserved a benefit in the asset concerned, these gifts are not treated as taxable for inheritance tax purposes as long as you survive for a period of seven years after making the gift. If you do not survive then the gift is added to the value of the estate upon your death. Taking this into account, it is therefore wise to consider giving away as much as you can. As far as larger gifts are concerned, it is also wise to consider whether or not the beneficiary is mature enough to cope with the size of the gift or whether it is prudent to put the gift into a trust, as described in the previous chapters.

The nil-rate band also operates in respect of lifetime gifts, with these being accounted for on a rolling seven-year basis. Should a gift become chargeable to IHT, either because it has been made during lifetime to a company or to a trust and the nil-rate band has been exceeded, or because you die within seven years, there are a number of reliefs and exemptions that apply. The most important of these is gifts in full to a UK domiciled spouse or to a registered civil partner. There are exemptions for gifts out of disposable income, (see below) gifts to political parties, charities and for national purposes. dispositions for the maintenance of family, small gifts of less than £250 per person per tax year and gifts in the occasion of the recipient's marriage. There is also an annual exemption of £3,000 per tax year which, if unused, can be carried forward to the next year (for one year only). It is therefore very important to have a firm grasp of gifts and exemptions in order to ensure that adequate planning takes place during your own lifetime.

Gifts out of excess income

There is a little-known option that involves making gifts from regular income to a loved one, which immediately become free of IHT. Some struggle to understand how it could work while others do not even know this valuable tax break exists.

Unlike other gifting options, there is no limit on the amount of excess income that can be gifted. Providing you have enough income left to meet your usual standard of living and spending needs, you can pass on as much as you wish within the exemption. How much will vary depending on your personal financial circumstances,

A parent or grandparent who wants to help a child or grandchild with their rent could potentially use this exemption, helping them out while reducing a future IHT bill. This exemption would allow them to offer more support than if they gave a lump sum or used another gifting allowance.

It needs to be done carefully, though, as you must meet certain criteria to avoid falling foul of HMRC. Payments must be from current income. This includes earned income, dividends, interest, rental income or pension income, rather than capital. Income saved from previous years may be deemed capital and is ineligible.

Gifts must come out of normal expenditure, rather than one-off sources of cash. You must have enough income to live on, with no negative impact on your standard of living after making the payment.

Gifts should also be consistent. HMRC will look for a pattern of payments over a reasonable period, typically of at least three to four years. However, they do not need to be the same amount on the same date. You must keep clear records of all gifts to show HMRC if requested. Making regular gifts from income could prove too expensive for many older people as living costs soar, but it does offer a valuable tax planning opportunity for those who can make the commitment.

Gifts with reservation of benefit and the pre-owned assets tax

A gift where you have reserved a right to benefit from the asset, for example, continued occupation of your house) may well be ineffective for the purposes of IHT. If there is to be no clean break it is vital that you take appropriate advice.

The existence of a number of schemes designed to get round the gifts with reservation of benefit rules led to the introduction of the 'pre-owned assets tax'. This pre-owned assets tax must be taken into account in any future planning.

Life assurance

Making contributions to a life policy is a very useful planning tool when considering future IHT liability, involving gifts. Policies are typically written in trust so that the proceeds do not form part of the policy holder's estate on death. This means that they can be used to provide for an IHT liability, either in respect of the full estate (whole of life policies) or in the case of death within seven years of making a gift (term assurance) without adding to the sum chargeable. The changes to the IHT trust regime introduced by the Finance Act 2006, however, can impact upon life policies and advice should be taken when large sums are involved.

There is also a wide range of investment products linked to life cover that form part of the IHT planning toolbox and that can again provide for a solution in the right circumstances. Again, more specialist advice should be taken in this area.

The family home

The family home represents probably the most sizeable chunk of most people's assets and will form the bulk of the estate. It is important that you have knowledge of the ways to treat the family home in respect of IHT.

When a property is owned by more than one person (for example husband and wife) that ownership can take one of two forms. A joint tenancy will mean that the property will pass automatically to the survivor on the death of a joint owner. A tenancy in common means that the share of each owner will pass according to the terms of their will (or if appropriate the rules of intestacy) A tenancy in common permits for more flexibility in dealing with the family home and for this reason a change in ownership might well be considered wise for IHT planning.

Gifting your home to your children

You may want to gift your home to a child. However, if you do this you should bear in mind that:

- gifts to your children-unlike gifts to your spouse or to your civil partner-aren't exempt from inheritance tax unless you live for seven years after making them

- if you keep living there without paying a full market rent it is not an 'outright gift' but a gift with reservation so its still treated as part of your estate and liable for IHT

- from 6th April 2005, you may be liable to pay an income tax charge on the benefit you get from having free or low-cost use of the property you formerly owned or provided funds to purchase
- Once you have given your home away your children own it and it becomes part of their assets, so if they are bankrupted or divorced the home may have to be sold to pay creditors or as part of a divorce settlement
- If your children sell your home, and it is not their main home, they will have to pay capital gains tax on any increase in value.

Downsizing to a smaller property

If you decide to downsize to a smaller property and give away the proceeds of the sale of the larger property, these gifts may qualify as:

- Potentially exempt transfers so they wouldn't be taxable unless you die within seven years
- Part of your annual exemption in £3000 chunks each year.

Given that your property probably forms the bulk of your estate it is essential that you know what you are going to do with it before HMRC takes a large slice of the value on death.

Wills and deeds of variation

One of the most important aspects of IHT planning is that of ensuring that you have a valid will in place. If you die without making a will your estate will be divided among family members according to the laws of intestacy. See chapter ten. Not only might this run totally counter to your wishes but it can also be very inefficient in terms of IHT planning. Have a will drawn up professionally, take expert advice. The costs are small compared with what might be at stake. Ensure that your will is subject to regular review. You should keep in mind that your will may cease to be valid if you marry or remarry.

If you die intestate or with a poorly devised will it is currently possible for relevant beneficiaries to enter into a deed of variation that, subject to time limits, can have the effect of putting things right for the purposes of IHT. A deed of variation is a document that alters a will posthumously and can be used to limit tax liability. It can be made at any time within two years of the death of the person who made the will and its purpose is to reduce IHT or capital gains tax, move assets into a trust, add a beneficiary who has been left out of a will or to correct an error. They are effective retrospectively from the time of death and any amendments are treated as though they are made by the deceased.

Wills Trusts and the equalisation of estates

Probably the most common IHT planning technique is the drafting of husband-and-wife wills to include a clause (typically establishing a Will Trust) that ensures that full use is made of the nil-rate band. If, on the first death, everything passes to a UK domiciled spouse there will be no IHT charge: however, on the second death the whole of the estate will be charged IHT. If, however, the first to die leaves a sum equivalent to the available nil-rate band to other beneficiaries there will still be no IHT payable and the joint estate is reduced by that sum.

Overall, therefore, both husband and wife will benefit from two nil-rate bands rather than just one-with a tax saving. However, planning of this sort must be accompanied by steps to ensure that the estates of husband and wife are equivalent to the extent that both include free assets at least to the value of the nil-rate band.

Deathbed planning

It should not be assumed that nothing can be done to plan or reduce IHT just because a person is elderly. Given the long life span, gifts in the hope of surviving seven years should not be ruled out. Sizeable gifts will benefit from the tapering of the associated IHT charge where the individual survives for more than three years. If survival for two years is a reasonable prospect, it may be considering a switch to investments that will enjoy business or agricultural property relief at the end of that period. Shares quoted on the Alternative Investment market (AIM) are an obvious option, with an increasing number of packaged products available. Even for those whose expectancy is measured in months rather than years it is important to review the position and ensure that there are no obstacles to obtaining relief. In limited circumstances there may be scope to change the status of assets to secure business or agricultural relief. Consideration should also be given to a number of investment base products that can achieve an IHT saving in this sort of situation.

Charity

Finally, if you intend to give the bulk of your estate to charity, it may be the case that you can forget about IHT. Do bear in mind however the other tax relief's that are available for lifetime charitable giving and the possibility that these may be used to boost your charitable giving further. In particular the creation of a charitable trust or foundation during lifetime may be an attractive proposition if you wish to donate considerable sums.

Rules affecting pensions

As mentioned previously, from April 2015, if a person dies before the age of 75, they can pass funds left in their pension to beneficiaries completely free of tax and no tax will be paid on the money that they withdraw from that pension. Previously, a punitive 55% was charged If a person dies after the age of 75 their beneficiaries will be able to draw on income from the pension pot, charged at their marginal rate (highest rate) of income, 20-40 or 45%. Alternatively, if they take the money as a lump sum, they will be taxed at 45%.

****

Chapter 9

Valuing an Estate and Applying for Probate

In this chapter we will look at the following:

- When to value an estate
- Assets of an estate
- Debts and liabilities
- Probate

This book is about inheritance tax, therefore one of the most important elements is that of the valuation of a person's estate, in order to ensure that you have an accurate idea of its worth and also of your inheritance tax liability. This topic was covered in the first few chapters but it is worth reiterating again within the context of the process of obtaining probate.

When valuing a deceased person's estate you must include property, possessions and money they owned at the time of their death, as well as certain gifts they may have made up to seven years before they died. Your valuation must reflect the current market value of the assets.

When you have to value an estate

Valuing the estate of someone who has died is one of the first things to do if you are acting as the executor or personal representative for the estate. You normally can't get access to the assets in the estate until you have received a grant of probate (or confirmation in Scotland). You need to know the estates worth to fill in the probate application form and show whether or not inheritance tax is due.

Assets of an estate

The assets of an estate are anything that has value, such as:

- money in accounts, building society, banks or other
- businesses or business assets owned by the deceased or a business partnership of which they were a member
- houses and land including farmland
- Stocks and shares
- Personal belongings such as antiques or jewellery
- Furniture and other fixtures in houses
- Motor vehicles
- Pensions that include a lump sum payment on death
- Assets in a trust from which the deceased benefited

- Life insurance payouts
- Other assets held abroad

The following should be evaluated to see if they are exempt:

- any assets given away in the seven years before death
- any asset that the deceased gave away at any time, but in which they retained an interest
- any assets jointly owned with someone else

Debts and liabilities

Debts and liabilities have to be balanced against assets. Liabilities include expenses from administering the estate. Examples include:

- mortgages outstanding
- debts on credit cards
- overdrafts
- unpaid taxes
- household bills
- outstanding loans
- funeral expenses

There are then a number of steps to take in arriving at the value of the estate.

a) Work out the market value of the assets and gifts

Finding out the market value of assets can be simple in some cases and more complicated in others. For example, you may need to use a surveyor to value property. You need to remember to include any gifts (money, property, or assets) that the deceased gave away that were not exempt. If you don't know the exact value of any item and the value of the estate is likely to be less than £200,000 then an accurate estimated figure will do.

Once you have completed this exercise you then add together the value of all the assets.

b) Deduct any debts

Deduct from the total market value of the assets anything that the deceased or the estate owed.

c) Make a record of the valuation

The value of all the assets minus all the debts is the value of the estate. These should be listed and a record kept of all the paperwork involved in the valuations should also be kept.

d) Decide if any heritance tax is due and which forms should be used. You will need different forms depending on where the deceased lived and whether inheritance tax is due. For a list of all the appropriate forms you should go to

HMRC website (address at back of the book which lists all the appropriate forms.

Inheritance tax and the probate process

Probate (or confirmation in Scotland) is the system you go through if you are handling the estate of someone who has died. It gives you the legal right to distribute the estate according to the deceased's wishes. Inheritance tax forms are part of the process even if the estate doesn't owe inheritance tax.

Probate terminology

If the deceased left a will, it would usually name one or more 'executors' who apply for grant of probate (also called a grant of representation).

If the deceased died without leaving a will, a blood relative can apply for a 'grant of letters of administration' depending on a strict next-of-kin order of priority defined in the rules of intestacy. This makes that person the administrator.

If the named executor doesn't want to act, someone else named in the will can apply to be the administrator (again depending on a strict order of priority).

Scotland and Ireland have their own terms, having different legal systems. The terminology is generally the same in Northern Ireland. However, in Scotland the process is called confirmation, and the personal representative applies for a grant of representation. Different forms are utilised in Scotland and Northern Ireland. The Northern Ireland Court Service website gives useful information on probate and other areas.

The process of probate

In England and Wales, the process is as follows:

- Value the estate as above and speak to the banks and other financial institutions to see whether you need probate
- If you need probate, complete the relevant probate and inheritance application forms-these differ depending on whether or not the estate owes inheritance tax
- Send the forms to the relevant government bodies. In England and Wales that's the controlling Probate Registry and HM Revenue and Customs (HMRC)
- Pay whatever inheritance tax is due
- Attend an interview at the Probate Registry and swear an oath
- Wait for the grant of probate to arrive in the post
- Pay any debts owed by the estate and then distribute the estate

Probate may not be needed if the estate:

- is a low-value estate-generally worth less than £5,000 and doesn't include land property or shares. In other words is low value and uncomplicated
- passes to the surviving spouse/civil partner because it was held in joint names.

You will almost certainly need probate if the estate includes:

- assets worth more than £5,000
- land or property in the name of the deceased, or held as tenants in common with someone else
- stocks or shares
- some insurance policies.

When applying for probate you will need to fill out an inheritance tax form in addition to the PA1 Probate Application form, even if the estate doesn't owe inheritance tax. The estate will only owe tax if it is over the threshold (£325,000 2023/24).

****

Useful addresses and websites

Inheritance tax

www.gov.co.uk/inheritance-tax

This is the official government website with a complete breakdown of inheritance tax.

HM Revenue and Customs (HMRC)
https://www.gov.uk/log-in-register-hmrc-online-services

This is the website of Her Majesty's Revenue and Customs with a complete breakdown of all allowances.

Probate

https://www.gov.uk/wills-probate-inheritance

Gives guidance on all matters concerned with probate

Also
London Probate Department
PRFD
First Avenue
42-49 High Holborn
Ground Floor

Holborn

London

WC1V 6NP

Tel: 0207 421 8509

****

Inheritance Tax

Glossary of terms

Accumulation

When the income of the fund is saved up and not paid out to any beneficiaries, it is said to be accumulated.

Administrator

A man who is appointed by the courts to administer a deceased person's estate in England, Wales and Northern Ireland; usually where there is no will or they are not named in the will.

Administratrix

A woman who is appointed by the courts to administer a deceased person's estate in England, Wales and Northern Ireland; usually where there is no will or they are not named in the will.

Agricultural relief

Relief from Inheritance tax that is due on the transfer of agricultural property. The relief applies to the agricultural value of the asset only.

Agricultural property.

Land or pasture used in the growing of crops or rearing of animals for food consumption, also can include farmhouses and farm cottages.

Agricultural value

The value a property would have if it could only be used as agricultural property.

Annual Exemption

The amount you can give away each tax year that will be exempt from Inheritance tax . This is currently £3,000 and applies to one gift or a number of gifts up to that amount.

Asset

A possession which has value, such as a house, land, cash or securities.

Beneficiary

For inheritance tax purposes, a beneficiary is a person or organisation which receives property, or gets some benefit from, a will, intestacy or trust.

Bereaved minor

A person who is aged under 18 and at least one of whose parents or step- parents has died.

Business

For the purpose of business relief, business includes any business carried on n the exercise of a profession or vocation.

Business relief

Relief from Inheritance Tax which is due on a transfer of relevant business property

Chargeable gift

From 22 March 2006, a chargeable gift is, broadly any gift that is not wholly covered by exemptions and given to the trustees of a relevant property trust or a company. Gifts from one individual to another or to disabled person's trust are not chargeable gifts, but are potentially exempt transfers.

Chargeable transfer

A transfer of value made by an individual which is not an exempt transfer.

Chargeable value

The chargeable value of an estate on death is the total of the asset less liabilities less exempt gifts and capital relief.

Charitable trust

A trust which is held indefinitely for charitable purposes only.

Charity exemption

A transfer that is made to a charity or other qualifying body is exempt from inheritance tax.

Chattels

Personal property such as household and personal goods, furniture, jewellery, antiques and works of art, stamp and coin collections, cars, caravans and boats, electrical, clothes, books, and garden equipment.

Consideration

A legal term meaning `something given for something done' i.e. the payment made for goods or services received. For a contract to be valid some consideration must be given.

Confirmation

The process of obtaining a grant of confirmation. In Scotland, England , Wales and Northern Ireland is known as probate .

Deed of Variation

See variation.

Deemed domicile

A legal concept for inheritance tax purposes where a person is treated as if they were domiciled in the UK at the time of a transfer if:

- they were domiciled in the UK within three years of the transfer, or
- they were resident in at least 17 of the last 20 years.
- **Dependant**
- A dependant of a registered pension scheme is defined as a person who at the time of the scheme member's death was
- the spouse or civil partner of the member
- a child of the member who was under 23
- a child of the member who was over 23 and in opinion of the scheme administrator was dependent on the member
- any other person who in the opinion of the scheme administrator was financially dependent on the member, had a financial relationship of mutual dependence with member, or was dependent on the member because of physical or mental impairment.

Disabled person

For inheritance tax purposes a disabled person is someone who, because of a mental disorder, is not capable of managing their own affairs or administering their own property or someone who is in receipt of attendance allowance or a disability allowance because they are entitled to the care component at the higher or middle rate.

Disabled person's interest Trust

A trust where more than half of the assets in the trust are applied for the benefit of a disabled person. Or, for trusts set up on or after 22 March 2006, a trust set up for their own benefit by a person who is suffering from a condition which can be expected to lead to them becoming disabled.

Discretionary trust

A trust under which no individual has a right to an interest in possession . generally , the trustees have the power to decide who should receive the capital or income from the trust. Discretionary trusts are also relevant property trusts.

Disposition

A disposal or transfer or property or cash, including both the creation and the release of any debt or right. The legislation specifically includes certain types of transfer and more information can be found in the Inheritance Tax Manual.

Domicile

Generally , a person's domicile is where they have their fixed and permanent home and to which, when they are absent, they always have the intention of returning.

Domicile of choice

Where a person has left their country of domicile to live in another country with the intention of settling permanently in the new country.

Domicile of dependency

Under the age of 16 a child has the same domicile as the person on whom they are legally dependent. This is called a domicile of dependency.

Domicile of origin

This is acquired by a child at birth and is usually the domicile of the child's father at that time . It need not be the country in which the child is born.

Donor

A person who makes a gift of some of their assets.

Donee

A person who receives a gift.

Double taxation convention (DTC)

A treaty which helps prevent a transfer from being taxed by two countries if both countries have the right to tax the same property when a death occurs or a gift is made.

Employee trust

A discretionary trust set up to benefit employees of a particular occupation or firm and the relatives and dependants of those employees.

Estate

Up to 22 March 2006, for inheritance tax purposes, a person's estate was made up of :

- assets in the sole name of the deceased,
- their share of any jointly owed assets,
- assets held in a trust in which the deceased had a right to benefit
- any nominated assets, and
- any assets they have given away, but kept an interest in (see gift with reservation) .

From 22 March 2006, a person's estate is made up of

- assets in the sole name of the deceased,

- their share of any jointly owed assets,
- assets held in trust in which the deceased had an immediate post - death interest, a disabled person's interest, or a transitional serial interest.
- Any `nominated assets,' and
- Any assets they have given away, but kept an interest in   (see gift with reservation).
- the value of an alternatively secured pension fund (ASP) from which the deceased benefited as the original scheme member, or as a dependant who received benefits from the left over ASP fund of the original scheme member.

In both cases, the total of all these assets is added to the chargeable value of any gifts made within seven years of the death to work out the amount on which tax is charged.

Excepted asset

An asset on which business relief is not available because it is not used wholly or mainly for the purposes of a business throughout the two years before a transfer.

Excepted estate

An estate where a full inheritance tax account is not required. From 6 April 2004 there are three types of excepted estate

- low value estates
- except estates
- foreign domiciles

Executor

A man who administers a deceased person's estate in England, Wales and Northern Ireland and is named in the will.

Executor- dative

A man who is appointed by the courts in Scotland to administer a deceased person's estate; usually where there is no will or they are not named in the will.

Executor- nominate

A man who administers a deceased person's estate in Scotland and is named in the will.

Executrices

Plural of executrix.

Executrix

A woman who administers a deceased person's estate in England, Wales and Northern Ireland and is named in the will.

Executrix- dative

A woman who is appointed by the courts in Scotland to administer a deceased person's estate; usually where there is no will or they are not named in the will.

Executrix- nominate

 A woman who administers a deceased person's estate in Scotland and is named in the will.

Exempt gifts

Gifts that are exempt from inheritance tax. These include

- gifts to individual more than seven years before death. See potentially exempt transfers.
- gifts to spouse or civil partners
- gifts not exceeding £3,000 in any one tax year. See annual exemption
- gifts on consideration of marriage or civil partnership
- gifts to UK charities
- gifts for national purposes
- small gifts
- gifts which are normal expenditure out of income.

Exempt transfer

An exempt transfer is one that is wholly covered by one or more exemptions.

Exemptions

Some gifts are exempt from inheritance tax because the gifts are covered by exceptions. See exempt gifts for details of the exemptions from inheritance tax that may apply.

Fall in value relief

When tax, or additional tax, is payable on a gift because the donor has died and the value of a gift has fallen between the date of the gift and the death, then tax is usually charged on the reduced value of the gift.

Gift in consideration of marriage or civil partnership

A gift made to a person who is about to get married or to form a civil partnership. These gifts are exempt from IHT up to the following amounts:

- £5,000 made by the person's parent
- £2,500 made by the person's grandparent
- £1,000 made by anyone else

Gift with reservation

See gift with reservation of benefit.

Gift with reservation of benefit

A gift which is not fully given away so that the person getting the gift does so with conditions attached or the person making the gift keeps back some benefit for themselves.

Grant of confirmation

The proof of legal authority required by the person who is entrusted with dealing with a deceased person's estate in Scotland.

Grant of double probate

A grant of representation where one executor dose not wish to prove the will and the right to join others later is reserved. When the non –proving executor withes to take up office later, a grant of double probate is made. Application for this is made on the form Cap A5C which is available from the Probate Registry.

Grant of representation

The proof of legal authority required by the person who is entrusted with dealing with deceased person's estate.

Grant of letters of administration

The proof of legal authority required by the person who is entrusted with dealing with a deceased person's estate where there is no will, or any will made is invalid.

Grant of letters of administration with will annexed

The proof of legal authority required by the person who is entrusted with dealing with a deceased person's estate where there is a will but no executor is named, or when the executors are unable or unwilling to apply for the grant.

Grant of probate

The proof of legal authority required by the person who is entrusted with dealing with deceased person's estate where there is a will.

Gross value of the estate

The total of all the assets that make up the deceased's estate before any of their debts are taken off.

Her Majesty's Revenue & Customs

The Government department created from the merger of the Inland Revenue and HM Customs & Excise.

IHT

Inheritance Tax

Immediately chargeable transfer

Before 22March 2006, there was an immediate claim for inheritance tax on gifts into discretionary trusts or to companies. For gifts made on or after 22 March 2006,an immediately chargeable transfer is one made to the trustees of a relevant property trust or to a company. Additional tax may be payable if the donor dies within seven years of the gift.

Immovable property
A person's possessions in the form interests in land and the permanent building on the land.

Inheritance Tax
A tax on the value of a person's estate on death and on certain gifts made by an individual during their lifetime.

Inheritance tax threshold
The inheritance tax threshold is the amount above which inheritance tax becomes payable. If the estate, including any assets held in trust and gifts made within seven years of death, is less than the threshold, no inheritance tax will be due on it.

Interest in possession
This is a term in general law. Generally, a person has an interest in possession in property held in trust if they have the immediate right to use or enjoy the property or receive any income arising from it. Up to 22 March 2006, all such trusts were treated for inheritance tax purposes as owned

by the person having the interest in possession. An interest in a trust arising on or after 22 March 2006 will be regarded as an interest in possession (and therefore treated for IHT purposes as owned by the person having an interest in possession) if it is one of the following:

- an immediate post-death interest
- a disabled person's interest
- a transitional serial interest

Intestate

If a person dies intestate, they died without making a will, or without fully disposing of their property by will. The administration of the estate is then governed by the provisions of the Administration of Estates Act 1925.

Intestacy

An estate where the person died intestate.

Inventory

Form C1 Confirmation with inventory is the form used for a Scottish estate on which the person's representative has to provide information such as assets of the estate, including assets situated outside of Scotland.

Joint asset

See joint property

Joint property

Something that is jointly owned by two or more people either as a `joint tenancy' or as `tenants in common'. Find out more about joint property in our guide to passing on your home to your children.

Joint tenancy

A form of joint ownership where all the joint owners have an identical interest in the property. On the death of the one owner, their interest passes to the remaining owner(s) by survivorship.

Life interest

A common form of interest in possession in settled property where a person has an interest for the duration of their lifetime.

Life tenant

A person who holds a life interest in settled property .

Limited probate

Where an executor is appointed in respect of certain assets only, such as literary works.

Loss to the estate

The value of a gift for inheritance tax purposes is the amount of the loss to the estate. It is worked out by looking at the value of the estate before and after the gift was made. The difference between those two figures is the loss in the estate.

Low value estates

A type of except estate where there can be no liability to inheritance tax because the total value of the estate, including the deceased's share of jointly owned assets, any specified transfer and specified exempt transfer, does not exceed the inheritance tax threshold.

Maintenance funds for historic lands & buildings

A type of discretionary trust set up for the maintenance of designated lands and buildings. Relief from full discretionary trust charges is available for these funds, but tax charge may arise if any property ceases to be held on the relevant trusts, or when the trustees make a disposition which reduces the value of the trusts.

Movable property

Goods, furniture and other items which can be moved from place to place.

National purposes

Exemption from inheritance tax is given for gifts and bequests to certain national institutions such as the National Gallery.

Newspaper trusts

Trusts set up for newspaper publishing companies or newspaper holding companies. These are treated like employee trusts for inheritance tax purposes.

Nil-rate band

The amount of an estate on which there is no inheritance tax to pay. If the value of an estate, including any assets held in trust and gifts made within seven years of death, falls within the nil – rate band there will be no IHT payable on the estate. Where the value of an estate exceeds the nil – rate band, only the amount above the nil –rate band is taxed at 40%.

Nominated asset

Certain assets, such as deposits with Friendly societies, National Savings Bank accounts and National Savings Certificates, can be transferred on death direct to chosen beneficiaries by nomination. Nominated property does not pass under the will or intestacy but it does form a part of the estate for inheritance tax purposes.

Nominee

A person who holds property on behalf of another.

Normal expenditure out of income

Gifts which are made purely out of income as part of a person's normal expenditure are exempt from inheritance tax. The claimant must show that after allowing for the gifts the donor was left with sufficient income to maintain their usual standard of living and that there was an established pattern of giving.

Notice of determination

A notice of determination may be issued where the personal representatives do not agree the value of the transfer. It is a written notice which states that the outstanding matters have been determined or payment of the outstanding tax has not been made. There is a right to appeal.

Open market value

For inheritance tax, the open market value of an asset is the price it might reasonably fetch if it was sold on the open market at the time of the transfer of that asset.

*

Outright gift

A gift where the donor gives away full ownership of the gift and does not retain any benefit.

Pecuniary legacy

A gift of a sum of money under a will.

Permanent home

The country where a person intends to live for the remainder of their life. It is the country whose laws decide, for example, whether a Will is valid, or how the estate of a person who has not made a Will is dealt with when they die.

Per stirpes

A property is to be divided `per stirpes' among the children of a deceased person, then each child takes an equal share. If a child has predeceased and the deceased that child's children will take equally between them the share that the predeceased child would have taken.

Personal applicant

A person who is applying for a grant of representation without the help of a solicitor or other agent.

PET

See potentially exempt transfer.

Political party

A gift to a political party qualifies to exemption from the inheritance tax if at the last general election preceding the transfer either two members of the party were elected to the House of Commons, or one member of the party was so elected and not less than 150,000 votes were given to candidates who were members of that party.

Potentially exempt transfer

Up to 22 March 2006, a potentially exempt transfer (PET) was an outright gift to an individual, to an accumulation and maintenance trust, or to a disabled person's interest, which becomes an exempt transfer if the donor lives for seven years after the date of the gift.

Power of attorney

An authority given by one person to another to act for him in their absence. The person authorised to act is the attorney of the other. See also enduring power of attorney.

Privileged will

A will made by a soldier on active service or a sailor at sea which does not have to comply with the usual formalities to make it valid. It does not have to be in writing, or, if it is in writing, does not have to be witnessed by two witnesses. The soldier or sailor can also be a minor.

Probate

Strictly, the exhibiting and proving of a will by the executors. In common usage as a general term describe the process of obtaining a grant of representation.

Property

The word `property' for inheritance tax purposes includes all types of asset, cash, stocks and shares etc as well as land and buildings, including all rights and interest of any description that are legally enforceable.

Proportionate charge

An inheritance tax charge on a relevant property trust (link to relevant property trust in the glossary) which arises when property in the trust ceases to be relevant property or when the trustees make a disposition which reduces the value of the relevant property.

The main examples of property ceasing to be relevant property are when the settlement comes to an end or when some of the property is distributed to beneficiaries.

Quick succession relief

See successive charges relief.

Related property

Related property is property that is in the estate of a spouse or civil partner, or belonging to a charity or one of the political, national or public bodies to which exempt transfers may be made. There are special rules for valuing related property.

Related settlement

When a settlor sets up a trust, any other trust he sets up on the same day are related settlements.

Relevant business property

Types of property on which business relief may be available. These include

- a business
- an interest in a Business, such as a partner
- unquoted shares which are not listed on recognised stock exchange
- shares or securities which give the transferor control of a business
- land, buildings, plant or machinery used wholly or mainly in the business or partnership

Relevant dependant

A relevant dependant of a member of a registered pension scheme is someone who at the date of the scheme member's death was

- a dependant who was the person's spouse or civil partner or
- is financially dependant on the member at the time.

Relevant property

Settled property held on a relevant property trust.

Relevant property trust

From 22 March 2006, a relevant property trust is any trust in which the beneficiary's interest is not one of the following:

- an immediate post – death interest
- a transitional serial interest
- a disabled person's interest
- a trust for a bereaved minor
- an age 18 to 25 trust

Relievable property

Property on which business relief or agricultural relief is available.

Resident

For inheritance tax purposes, residence has the same meaning as for income tax purposes. To be regarded as resident in the UK you must normally be physically present in the country at same time in the tax year. You will always be resident if you are here for 183 days or more in the tax year.

Residue

The part of an estate which is left after the payment of specific and pecuniary legacies, debts, funeral expenses and IHT.

Restriction on disposal

The value of an asset may be reduced if the right to dispose of it is restricted.

Reversionary Interest

The future right to an interest in settled property.

Settled property-See settlement.

Settlement

A settlement occurs when property is held in trust for successive beneficiaries . The property which a settlor puts into trust is known as the trust fund or` settled property'.

Settlor

A person who puts property into trust. For inheritance tax purposes a settlor is the person who makes a settlement or who directly or indirectly provides the assets for a settlement.

Simultaneous deaths

For inheritance tax, if two or more people die and it is not known who died first, we assume that they have died at the same moment. This does not alter the legal position for the administration of the estate which is that the elder is presumed to have died first.

Small gifts

Small gifts which are exempt from inheritance tax of up to £250 in each tax year to any number of different recipients. The exemption cannot be combined with any other exemption such as the annual exemption.

Special Commissioners

The Special Commissioners hear and determine appeals concerning decisions of the Inland Revenue relating to all direct taxes including income tax, corporation tax, capital gains tax and inheritance tax.

Special Trust

Types of discretionary trusts where the settled property held on them is not relevant property.

Special gifts

A gift other than a gift of residue Typical specific gifts are pecuniary legacies, gifts of particular assets such as the deceased's residence, furniture, jewellery and other household and personal goods and effects or shares in companies and business assets.

Specified exempt transfers

Gifts other than the deceased's spouse or civil partner charities, political parties, housing associations, maintenance funds for historic buildings and employee trusts must be added back to see if the estate qualifies as an excepted estate.

Specified transfers

Gifts of cash, chattels or corporeal movables, quoted shares or securities, or outright gifts of land or buildings to individuals, not gifts into trust. For an estate to qualify as excepted estate (excepted estate), specified transfer made within 7 days of death cannot exceed £100,000.

Spouse

A person who is legally married to someone else.

Spouse or civil partner exemption

Gifts made between spouses or civil partners are exempt from inheritance tax. This exemption is limited to £55, 000 if the deceased (or donor) was domiciled in the UK and their spouse or civil partner was not domiciled in the UK at time of the transfer.

Successive charges relief

A relief designed to reduce the burden of IHT where an estate taxable on death reflects the benefit of property received within the previous five years under a transfer on which tax was (or becomes) payable.

Surviving civil partner

A person whose civil partnership has ended through death of their civil partner.

Survivorship

Where property is owned jointly under a joint tenancy, on the death of one of the joint tenants, the deceased's share of the joint property passes automatically to the surviving joint tenant(s). The property cannot be passed to anyone else under a will or intestacy.

Taper relief

If the total chargeable value of all the gifts made between three and seven years before death is more than the threshold at death, then taper relief is due. The relief reduces the amount of tax payable on a gift, not the value of the gift itself.

Ten – yearly charge

An inheritance tax charge which arises on a relevant property trust on the tenth anniversary of the setting up of the trust and each subsequent ten- yearly anniversary.

Tenants in common

Joint ownership of property where each joint tenant owns a separate share in the property. On the death of one of the joint owners, their share passes to their beneficiaries by their will or intestacy.

Testator

A man who has made a will. A Testatrix is a woman who has made a will

Transfer

Inheritance tax is charged on a transfer of value. That transfer can occur either during a person's lifetime, in the form of a gift, or on a person's death.

Transferee

A person who receives a transfer.

Transferor

A person who make a transfer.

Trust

An obligation binding a person who holds the legal title, the trustee, to deal with the property for the benefit of another person; the beneficiary

Trust fund-See settlement

Trustee

The person who holds the legal title to settled property and who is obliged to deal with the property for the benefit of the beneficiaries.

Trust for a bereaved minor

A trust for a bereaved minor is a trust which is exempt from mainstream inheritance tax charges if it is held either:

- on the statutory trust applying to minor children aged up to 18 on intestacy or
- on trusts in similar terms established under the terms of a parent's will or by the Criminal Injuries Compensation Scheme.

Trust for disabled people

A discretionary trust set up for the benefit of a disabled person. After 9 March 1991 these trust were treated as if the disabled person had an interest in possession in the property held in the trust. Any distributions from the trust to the disabled person are not taxable, but a charge to IHT will arise on their death and the trust fund will form part of their estate.

Unilateral Relief

Where a transfer is liable to Inheritance Tax and also to similar tax imposed by another country on assets situated in that country with which the UK does not have a double taxation agreement, relief may be available under unilateral relief provisions.

Variation

If all of the original beneficiaries agree, an inheritance under a will   or under an intestacy can be changed after death.

Will

The legal document by which a person declares their intention as to what should happen to their estate after their death.

Woodlands relief

When a woodland in the United Kingdom is transferred on death, the person who would be liable for the tax can elect to have the value of the trees and under wood (but not underlying land) excluded from the deceased's estate. If the timber is later disposed of its value at the time will be subject to inheritance tax.

****

Index

****

www.straightforwardbooks.co.uk

All titles, listed below, in the Straightforward Guides Series can be purchased online from Amazon.

Law

A Straightforward Guide to:

Healthcare Law for Patients, Carers and Practitioners

Criminal Law

Consumer Rights

Bankruptcy Insolvency and the Law

Public Law

Business law

Employment Law

Private Tenants Rights

Family law

Small Claims in the County Court

Contract law

Intellectual Property and the law

Divorce and the law

Leaseholders Rights

The Process of Conveyancing

Knowing Your Rights and Using the Courts

Producing Your own Will

Housing Rights

The Bailiff the law and You

Being a Litigant in person

Probate and The Law

Company law

What to Expect When You Go to Court

Rights of Disabled Children

Rights of Disabled people

Give me Your Money-Guide to Effective Debt Collection

Guide For the Litigant in person

General titles

Letting Property for Profit

Buying, Selling and Renting property

Buying a Home in England and France

Bookkeeping and Accounts for Small Business

Creative Writing

Freelance Writing

Writing Your own Life Story

Writing performance Poetry

Writing Romantic Fiction

Kate Walkers 12 Point Guide to Writing Romance

Speech Writing

Teaching Your Child to Read and write

Teaching Your Child to Swim

Raising a Child-The Early Years

Creating a Successful Commercial Website

The Straightforward Business Plan

The Straightforward C.V.

Successful Public Speaking

Handling Bereavement

Individual and Personal Finance

Understanding Mental Illness

****